TEACHER / SWIMMER

"The Mind-Body Connection"
Addressing the Needs
of the Fearful Swimmer

by JOHN NEUNER

ACKNOWLEDGMENTS

To my wife, Barbara, who has given me unwavering support and assistance throughout the process of writing **Teacher/Swimmer.** She is a very special friend.

To my sister-in-law, Marilyn Klein, who painstakingly took the time to edit my original manuscript and subsequent revisions. I feel privileged to have such a talented lady in my family. I have learned so much about writing from her.

To my son, Matt, who was my illustrator. He is a great listener and has the uncanny ability to visually reproduce what he hears described to him. He tied it all together for me. I cannot think of a better qualified person for this job.

To my son, Eric, who as a young boy never let me forget the importance of supervision whenever a child is playing in or near the water.

To my dog, Belmont (1981-1998), who was always at my side whenever I was writing **Teacher/Swimmer.**

To Abner E. Kohn, my publisher, for believing in the message I am trying to convey in **Teacher/Swimmer.** His insights were invaluable and focused.

To my many friends who took the time to read my manuscript at various points in its development. I dare not mention names for fear of forgetting someone. You know who you are and I thank you.

TABLE OF CONTENTS

INTRODUCTION

Throughout the ages people have drowned because of sudden unexpected situations requiring minimal swimming skills or precautions to save oneself: the fisherman who falls off a dock, the teenager who slips into a pool, the child who is insensitively pushed or thrown into the water, the boy who jumps off a bridge. (As well as those courageous people who drown trying to save them.)

From the **New York Times,** June 30, 1996:
"Screams and sobs echoed through the vaulted nave of St. Francis of Assisi Church in the Crown Heights section of Brooklyn yesterday as hundreds of mourners gathered for the funeral of Marc C. Britou Jr., a 13-year old honors student, who drowned last weekend while on a school trip."

Mayor Rudolph Guiliani delivered the eulogy, expressing these sentiments: *"This loss of yours, this tragedy of yours, touches all the people of New York City. . . .He was a fine young man, he was a good student with any number of things lying ahead for him - a great future, a great career."*

Marc's math teacher was quoted as saying, "You know, a lot of times when a kid dies, people say they were good when they weren't. This is a legitimate case of a really good kid, always happy, always helping other students."

Marc Britou was part of a group of students attending Intermediate School 61 who went on a field trip to the Franklin Institute, a Philadelphia science museum, sponsored by Medgar Evers College. The field trip was a reward for the students who scored well on the New York State High School Regents Biology examination. The students had attended an after-school program for the purpose of preparing for this examination.

The group of thirteen students and seven chaperones had returned to the Travelodge hotel in South Philadelphia to rest up before dinner. Shortly before 7:00 PM, Marc Britou, Jason Moore, a boy by the name of Damion and a fourth teenager went into the pool area.

"The four of us were in the pool," Damion explained. "The water was cold so we were hanging onto the edge."

Damion swam into the deep water, followed by Jason Moore. Jason tried to stand up – not realizing he was over his head in deep water. Jason began to drown and called to Damion for help. Damion and Marc swam over to Jason and tried to help him. Both Marc and Jason could barely swim.

There was no lifeguard. The clarity of the water was described as "murky." The guests of the hotel sitting by the pool thought that the boys were just fooling around. According to Damion, the boys did not realize that they were in deep water. By the time everyone realized that Jason was in serious trouble, the courageous Marc Britou, in the confusion, had slipped under the water and drowned. It was not until minutes later when someone, using a long pole to probe the bottom of the pool, discovered the lifeless body of Marc Britou. Jason Moore died ten days later.

"Where were the teachers?" Where was the supervision? Without warning, tragedy changed joyous, caring, and well-intentioned relationships into bitter and angry ones. The assignment of blame became the focus of discussion.

But there were questions that, inexplicably, I have never heard asked, and issues that are never adequately addressed:

"Why did these two bright young responsible teenagers not have the minimal water competency skills to save themselves?"

"Why are we as an enlightened society not mandating the teaching of minimal water competency skills in order to empower and protect our young?"

Consider these facts (*from the National Safe Kids Campaign*):
Drowning is the *second* leading cause of unintentional injury-related death among children ages 14 and under.

Older children are more likely to drown in open water sites, such as lakes, rivers and oceans.

In 1995, more than *1,000 children,* ages 14 and under, drowned. For every child who drowns, an additional four are hospitalized for near-drowning; and for every hospital admission, approximately four children are treated in hospital emergency rooms.

Fifteen percent of children admitted for near-drowning die in the hospital. As many as twenty percent of near-drowning survivors suffer severe, permanent neurological disabilities.

Male children have a drowning rate two to four times that of female children.

In general, black children, ages 14 and under, have a drowning death rate that is two times greater than white children.

Low income children are at greater risk from non-swimming pool drownings.

Typical medical costs for a near-drowning victim can range from **$75,000** for initial emergency room treatment to **$180,000** a year for long-term care. The cost of near-drowning that results in brain damage can be more than **$4.5 million.**

The total annual cost of drownings and near-drownings among children under the age of 14 is approximately **$6.2 billion.**

A Florida survey, reported by the **New York Daily News** on June 30, 1996, revealed that 80% of that state's **drowning** victims were black or a member of a minority group. Statistics from the U.S. Military Academy indicated that 90% of the white cadets could swim by the age of 9, compared with 58% of the entering black cadets from urban areas. In contrast, black cadets from middle-class suburbia had higher numbers of swimmers. *(Children who are not taught to swim at an early age tend to grow either fearful or dangerously overconfident about their ability.)*

In the **Daily News** report, Jenny Morgenthau, executive director of the Fresh Air Fund recalled one youngster who jumped into a pool and sunk to the bottom. After being pulled out he sputtered, "I didn't know it would be so hard."....Many children have been lured into a false sense of security because they have spent time standing in 3 or 4 foot **city** pools crowded wall to wall-with-other children."They think that is swimming."

City Parks Commissioner Henry Stern, according to the **Daily News,** estimated that fewer than half the children who use the city's pools know how to swim.

WAKE-UP CALL

The evidence is abundantly clear. Too many young people are at risk of drowning when they go "swimming." The question is: Why? More importantly, how can we combat this problem. The most obvious answer is education, which must start somewhere. It begins by educating the individual to better understand the water experience.

Teacher/Swimmer provides information that enables the readers to protect themselves as well as those the readers must protect. The information is both philosophical and practical, and when you understand, appreciate and absorb the process, you are in a better position to execute the skills being taught – not only in swimming but also in a wide range of life-threatening situations.

Non-swimmers will gain empowering insights into the water experience; swimmers will become sensitized to the problems and anxieties facing non-swimmers.

Most people who drown never expected to be in the water. Many never expected to be in water over their heads. **Teacher/Swimmer** *focuses on the skills that are necessary to swim only that short distance to safety if you should suddenly and unexpectedly find yourself in deep water.*

OVERVIEW

From the Spring of 1983 to June of 1992, I was privileged to work as a full-time swimming teacher of children ranging in age from 8-13 years at PS32 in the Bronx. Working as a swimming teacher gave me the unique opportunity to improve the quality of life for many young children in a dramatically positive way. What my job lacked in prestige and acknowledgment was overwhelmingly made up for with pride, satisfaction, and student appreciation.

Teacher/Swimmer is a conversational "How To" program based upon my experiences as a New York City public school swimming teacher. The contents of the program consist of the methods, skills, reasoning and concepts that I attempt to convey to my students. The information is presented in the simplest of terms since, in essence, the program should be viewed as a *water competency primer.*

Teacher/Swimmer is not just a swimming program about how the body moves in water, it also a program about how the *mind* can either **positively** or **negatively** impact movement itself.

Teacher/Swimmer stresses the *incremental* skills that *cumulatively* make a learner water competent. My approach is to focus on a few simple concepts and skills, while compensating for the potential redundancy of the message by continuously striving to maintain a comfortable, positive, fun and upbeat environment. In essence, my program is narrow in focus. *The goal is to facilitate the positive connection of the mind with the body that conditions these young people not to panic when faced with a crisis situation.*

Teacher/Swimmer focuses on the gross motor execution of a swimming stroke as opposed to the finer nuances. Correct swimming form is more **efficient** but not necessarily more **effective** than less correct swimming form. A person falling into the water suddenly and unexpectedly can save himself/herself in a number of different ways. Effectiveness far outweighs form in terms of priorities at this elementary level of water competence.

The main objective of **Teacher/Swimmer** is to present learning how to swim as a *life* skill, not a *competitive* skill. The approach is similar to running in a marathon event. For most runners, it is getting there that counts. Winning is an *external* goal that is reserved for a select group of athletes with God-given skills. Getting there is an *internal* goal belonging to all participants.

Teacher/Swimmer is in no way intended to supplant the teachings of the Red Cross and other organizations that have led the charge in trying to promote water safety. From the beginning, Red Cross publications have been a valuable source of technical information and teaching support. I could not have done my job effectively without referring to these publications. It is my intention to continually look to the Red Cross for guidance, assistance and leadership. I recommend that my readers look to this and other organizations for formal swimming lessons.

THE TEACHER/SWIMMER

Is the reader up for the challenge? Webster defines "to teach" as follows: *To impart instruction to; to guide the studies of; to instruct; to impart the knowledge of; to instruct, train or give skill in the use, management, or handling of; to let be known; to tell; to show how; to show.*

Nowhere does it say that you must be licensed! Nowhere does it say you must be an expert! If you can swim or at least understand the mechanics of swimming, you can teach swimming. **If you are sensitive to the process of learning how to swim, you can be a** *teacher/swimmer.*

A **teacher/swimmer** attempts to demystify learning how to swim. A **teacher/swimmer** views learning how to swim no differently than learning how to play baseball. Concerned parents and volunteers have done a remarkable job of teaching young children to throw, catch, and hit for generations, realizing that this is a step by step process. A coach can lead a young player up many steps before the services of an expert is needed.

Is it not possible for the **teacher/swimmer** to model such an approach with the non-swimmer? The **teacher/swimmer** can teach the skills that eventually lead the learner to achieve water competence. The **teacher/swimmer** facilitates the connection of the mind with the body. The ability to swim is a skill. The ability to teach is an art. *The teacher/swimmer is a person who blends the ability to teach with the skills needed to swim.*

TEACHERS

Great teachers are great students. They have the confidence to admire and not begrudge other masters of their trade. It is not important that a **teacher/swimmer** be a storehouse of knowledge. Rather, it is the ability to *convey* that knowledge which qualifies one to be a **teacher/swimmer**.

As the expression goes **"Those that can't do, teach."** And, I believe there is a very powerful germ of truth here in the sense that those who are able to master skills at a level reserved for a select few find it very difficult, if not impossible, to understand the frustrations and struggles of the learner. On the other hand, "non-olympians" are in a better position to connect and empathize with the learner.

LEARNERS

Learners fall somewhere along a continuum: Below Average – Average – Above Average. The above average learner succeeds no matter who the **teacher/swimmer** is because his/her mind-body connection is finely tuned. It all comes so easy. On the other hand, the below average learner must always deal with frustration. The mind and body are often out of synch and so for this learner nothing comes easy. Teaching success hinges on the understanding that all learners are different.

THE RUSH

During my 10 years as a **teacher/swimmer,** I can conservatively estimate that over 1,000 frightened non-swimmers became swimmers as a result of my efforts. These learners reached a level of efficacy, self-realization and **water competency** usually reserved for people living in a more privileged non-urban environment. They were learners who made the mind-body connection. *It is safe to say that few of them will panic and drown if they find themselves suddenly and unexpectedly in deep water.*

There is a coaching term: **"You must always be in the game"** – totally involved - totally committed. The **teacher/swimmer** views learners frolicking in the water as a theater of learning opportunities, sensing those special moments when a beginner is ready to take that next step up the ladder of water competency. Seizing that moment, helping the learner take that step and to be rewarded only by that special look that says," **I did it!**" It is a rare privilege to share a moment of triumph with a young person and to always occupy a special place in his/her memory.

I like to call it the **teacher/swimmer** "*RUSH.*" Teaching the beginning swimmer gives it to you in steady doses!

I welcome the reader to learn to become a **teacher/swimmer.**

John Neuner
March 1998

TEACHER / SWIMMER

Photo of John Neuner's son, Eric, diving off a rock in City Island, Bronx, NY, at the age of four, vividly reminds Mr. Neuner of his own youth, whereby swimming and water play were his primary sources of fun and pleasure. His perspective of swimming formulated as a child strongly influences his approach to teaching swimming as an adult. *Photo by George Zanicchi in 1980.*

1
MY UNUSUAL JOURNEY

There are those who say I could swim before I could walk. This may be true, but the real reason I suspect is because I was a late walker. Other children my age were already running while I was still crawling. I cannot remember, however, not knowing how to swim, or walk, for that matter. Growing up in a waterfront community on Long Island Sound, water was my life. It seemed that all activities were somehow water-related: boating, fishing, clamming, swimming, snorkeling and employment opportunities. My community, City Island in the Northeast Bronx (borough of New York City), was once considered the yachting capital of the world.

There were some interesting anomalies regarding the children growing up on City Island. Everybody loved the water and everyone, it seems, knew how to swim. Very few residents ever went for formal swimming instruction. Oddly enough, only a handful of the children went on to swim competitively on high school swim teams. The simple truth is that City Island children did not perform well according to "correct form" standards.

True, we were water-competent without many irrational fears of the water. But, we were not great swimmers using traditional norms. More importantly, however, we knew our limitations and had tremendous common sense around the water. As a matter of fact, I cannot remember anyone drowning because of not knowing how to swim. Water competency required us to adapt to the potential hazards in our swimming environment. Experientially, we could instinctively measure the risks. To this day, I have an aversion to diving vertically into the water. Due to a lack of water clarity in many areas where I swam, large rocks ominously greeted the unsuspecting diver.

Growing up, I was considered one of the better swimmers in my age group – the ability to swim fast was the measure of relative ability. I guess it is the same anywhere you go, competition always seems to prevail.

My greatest childhood swimming accomplishment was swimming from Rat Island to City Island at the age of seven - a 400 yard swim. Rat Island is a small island east of City Island. I was accompanied by my mother and brother in a small boat and used a combination of "doggie-paddle" and overhand arm strokes. (Rudimentary but effective!)

Risk assessment and risk management are vital components of water competency. I instinctively knew at an early age that attempting this 400 yard swim alone without someone watching me was inherently dangerous and foolhardy. No explanations from the adults were needed. It was simply out of the question. The element of common sense around the water is what separates water competency from the mechanics of swimming.

My family were water people. We all loved just being in and around the water, spending numerous hours diving, swimming, relaxing, and playing. While out in a boat we would stop the engine in the middle of Long Island Sound and dive or jump into the water. We were exhilarated by the special foreboding thrill of jumping off a boat and swimming in the middle of the Sound, the further away from land the better!

A special day would be to visit one of the beaches on

the South Shore of Long Island and to swim in the ocean or to take a boat ride to the North Shore of Long Island and spend an overnight at one of the sandy beaches. Water and water related activities were the focus of our lives.

Probably my love of the water began with my mother. I never knew anyone who loved the water more. She spent her summers growing up in "Tent City," which was a small summertime community on Rodman's Neck on the Bronx mainland across from City Island. Tent City was demolished in the 1930's and replaced with what is now Orchard Beach. My mother's family moved to City Island at that time.

Some of my fondest memories were taking boat rides with my mother in her final years and discussing how life on the waterfront had changed over time. Mom was great company and even though her body was failing her, she was always young at heart. There was always a certain sadness, however, because although we never discussed it, we both knew we did not have that much more time together. A chapter of our lives was ending.

Unfortunately, in the final years of her life, my mother was in and out of the hospital due to chronic emphysema. She lived less than a block away from the water and swam every day, weather permitting. When, as it turned out, she was going into the hospital for the last time, she was much too weak to walk to the beach. Undaunted, she drove her car down the short block to take her last "dip" in the cool waters of Long Island Sound. Somehow, I think Mom knew she would never return to her beloved water. She passed away less than a week later.

At the age of 16, I enrolled in the Lifeguard Training Program conducted by the New York City Department of Parks. I found the situation quite intimidating, feeling insecure compared to the other students. They were "pool" people and I was not. I was a boy who grew up on an island

and my experiences were very different from theirs.

The majority of lifeguard candidates were trained swimmers and most swam competitively on High School swim teams. I was someone who knew how to swim but prior to my lifeguard training, I had never had any kind of formal swim training whatsoever. I basically knew only what my parents had taught me. I picked up other swimming skills, many of which were non-traditional, on my own.

My feelings were internal and were never verbalized. The teachers in the school and my fellow students were friendly and never realized how different I felt. Despite my feelings of insecurity, however, I was able to perform all the skills and requirements necessary to complete the lifeguard training course successfully.

Working as a lifeguard at Orchard Beach in the Bronx for five seasons was my first introduction to the non-swimmer. Orchard Beach is a man-made beach about a mile long from jetty to jetty. Although it is located on Long Island Sound, it did not have many of the obvious perils one would experience while swimming in the ocean. For the most part, Orchard Beach was calm and non-threatening. There were dangers, however, lurking for the unsuspecting non-swimmer. We called them the "**drops.**"

THE DRÒPS

Because of tidal movements, storms, erosion, and other environmental factors, the sand would abruptly drop off, creating a shelf. *The drops would occur where the beach ended and the underwater portion of Long Island Sound began. (Drops can also be experienced in lakes, rivers and oceans.)* The drops could be so severe at times that a person standing in waist high water would dive forward and end up over his/her head. The swimming area at high tide was spacious and safe with plenty of swimming room and no drops. The situation changed dramatically, however, at low tide. The distance from the water's edge to the drops was only about 30 feet in some sections. All the bathers were now confined to a smaller swimming area.

THE TREACHEROUS "DROPS"

There were hot low tide afternoons – especially during full moons – when all we did was rescue unsuspecting bathers. It was both exciting and frightening. The responsibility at times felt overwhelming.

Our eyes remained riveted to the water. We developed uncanny instincts. An errant splash, seen through our peripheral vision, would send a lifeguard flying off the chair in the direction of a drowning victim. Many times I found myself running into the water, saving a drowning victim, and not realizing what I saw before I left the chair.

My experience as a lifeguard helped me to develop skills and instincts that later proved invaluable when I became a swimming teacher. They include:

•   Never take your eyes away from the water. There is no substitute for supervision.

•   Fear causes panic to the point where the drowning

victims are totally incapable of helping themselves. They cannot even call for help.

• The physical, psychological and emotional responses to a drowning situation varies from victim to victim.

• Inexperienced swimmers sometimes totally forget how to swim when faced with what they see as a crisis situation. I have seen swimmers swimming along quite competently until they realize they are in water over their heads. Panic sets in and the drowning process begins. The reaction can be sudden or in stages.

• Take nothing for granted. I have seen drowning victims go into shock and stop breathing even **after** being rescued.

• There are always tell-tale signs which convey that something is wrong: the look in the eyes, the splashing of the arms. Anticipate and react to the situation immediately.

My Aunt Jane worked for the New York City Board of Education. The year was 1971 and I was a Physical Education teacher at the time. Aunt Jane would always be looking out for her son, my cousin, Richie, and myself. She would never forget to call my mother with any information she considered important. She was our pipeline to the Board, and that was how we learned about its swimming teacher examination.

This examination was offered every few years. The swimming teacher license was coveted by those people concerned with securing after-school work. Back in those years, recreation opportunities for the children were considered a priority. Schools, pools and other facilities were open afternoons, nights, and weekends in order to give young people something to do.

My reaction was that the idea was ridiculous. I never swam competitively and did not know the first thing about pools. I had never had any formal instruction other than lifeguard training. **What qualified *me* to be a swimming**

teacher? Take the swimming teacher examination? Out of the question! My feelings were relayed to my Aunt Jane by my mother. A few days later an application arrived in the mail. When the application arrived, I ignored it. For some foolish reason, I thought my Aunt Jane would forget about the application as well. A few days before the application was due, my Aunt Jane called my mother to find out if I had sent in my swimming teacher application. So naturally, I sent it in. I could not believe the absurdity of the situation. How was I going to pass a swimming teacher examination?

The swimming teacher examination included a performance test and a written test. I never believed for a second I could pass the written test; I had limited pool experience and training. I did have a friend, however, who was a swimming teacher in a local high school. She lent me a book on how to teach swimming.

I read the book looking for key words and phrases. Amazingly, I passed the written test using a combination of common sense, teaching experience, lifeguard experience, and the newly acquired swimming vocabulary that I learned from the book. Mind you, I did not pass the written test with flying colors. But I passed!. Soon thereafter, I became a licensed New York City Board of Education swimming teacher.

Due to a series of unplanned events I became a full time day swimming teacher at PS32 in 1981. Located in the Belmont section of the Bronx, PS32 was a 4th-6th grade school made up of inner-city children ranging in ages from 8-13. The ethnically mixed enrollment included up to 900 students with a well integrated mix of regular as well as special education classes. The existence of a swimming pool in an elementary school was unusual, to say the least. A more apropos description was that it was unheard of!

The PS32 pool was built in the 1930's. It is a ground

level facility, one story high, with two magnificent skylights directly over the pool itself. The dimensions of the pool are 18' x 40' with a shallow end of 3 feet in depth, and a gradually sloping bottom to a deep end of 7 feet in depth. The entire pool and deck flooring are made of meticulously placed one-inch tile. There is a locker room, a shower room and an office. The office has windows facing the pool and sides allowing for optimum safety and visibility. It is a well designed facility reflecting the craftsmanship of a bygone era.

From a professional perspective my position was teaching *Nirvana*! The district administrations were enlightened enough to see the intrinsic benefits of having a swimming program in an elementary school. There was a cherished tradition of children living in the community learning how to swim in the PS32 pool. The principal believed in it and the custodian was allotted extra money for it. It was a perquisite unique to the Belmont community.

To the best of my knowledge, I was the third person ever to have this position on a full-time basis. The original teacher was there over 40 years. The second teacher assumed the position when he was in his late 50's and worked as a swimming teacher for less than 10 years. I assumed the position when he retired.

There was no swimming curriculum as such, since there were no guidelines about how to teach swimming in an elementary school with a swimming student to teacher ratio of 800:1. An enrollment of 800-900 children did not allow for any real degree of concentrated individualized teaching. It was an awesome challenge embellished with unparalleled freedom.

PRIVILEGED VS UNDERPRIVILEGED

The majority of children attending PS32 were underprivileged. More privileged children live for the most part in structured communities where recreation and learning op-

portunities abound. They attend summer camps and there is
an infrastructure of organizations and facilities which are
conducive to personal development. Density of population
is an important factor since, if fewer people live in a community, there are inherently more opportunities available to
each member. Learning how to swim can easily become
part of each child's education, both formally and informally.

Underprivileged children, on the other hand, live in
communities that are, for the most part, unstructured. Except for schools, churches and community organizations, there
is insufficient infrastructure to deal with many quality-of-
life issues.

Underprivileged children are not privy to many of
the life experiences that more privileged children take for
granted, learning to swim being one of those experiences.
Their parents, frequently, are not water competent since they,
too, come from underprivileged backgrounds. Hence, the
problem now becomes generational. *The presence of a pool
in an elementary school in an underprivileged area presents
a swimming teacher with a very special as well as unique
mission.*

IRONY

Working as a lifeguard at Orchard Beach in the Bronx,
I witnessed the perils facing the non-swimmer up close for
five seasons. I was involved in saving close to 150 swimmers in routine drowning situations, situations requiring
minimal skills to save oneself. These situations could have
led to death by drowning, if it were not for outside intervention. Such irony! Here I was **16 years later, teaching the
same population I had saved 16 years earlier how to swim.
I felt uniquely qualified since I had witnessed their deep-
est fears first hand. I relished the challenge of equipping
these children with the skills to save their lives.**

MISSION STATEMENT

It was quite apparent from the very beginning that my primary mission as a teacher/swimmer was to teach a learner how to become water competent. By water competency, I mean the development of skills, attitudes and strategies which allow a learner to effectively manipulate the water environment. Water competency involves enabling the learner to get in touch with the mind-body connection, whereby certain responses become instinctive and ingrained in the psyche. This allows the learner to develop the ability to recognize and react appropriately to any situation that threatens the health and welfare of the learner, as well as others.

Water competency gives you a chance to **think.** Not just to think, but to think clearly. The ability to think clearly enables you to assess, to plan, to realize your options and limits, and to take action. It enables you to tap into a pool of common sense knowledge no matter what your predisposition is in a crisis situation.

BOTTOM LINE

There are sudden unexpected events that can occur in life whereby a person may find himself/herself over the head in a body of water and must swim a short distance to safety. A person may slip or be pushed into a pool or fall off a pier or dock. There are innumerable possibilities and scenarios. The issue is that in the majority of cases **minimal** skills are required in order to save oneself. Due to inexperience and fear, however, the victim panics and drowns. *My mission is to watersafe my learners to the point, where, if one of my learners ends up in deep water as a result of a sudden unexpected event, he/she will not panic and drown.*

2
THE MIND-BODY
CONNECTION

The success or failure of any water competency program demands that we focus on the "**whole**" learner. That is, we must focus on all of the tangibles as well as the intangibles when teaching water competency. Our expectations must vary from learner to learner. *The teacher/ swimmer focuses on the process, which, in turn, allows the product to take on its own special form.*

Each human being is unique. There are a whole number of physical, intellectual, psychological, emotional, social, familial and experiential factors contributing to this uniqueness. It is not necessarily the role of the teacher/ swimmer to deal with these problems in a clinical sense. Rather, it is necessary for the teacher/swimmer to be aware of these factors to better understand the needs of the learner. *Understanding the needs of the learner is the driving force behind the achievement of positive outcomes.*

THE MIND-BODY CONNECTION

Learning how to swim has as much to do with the mind as it does with the body. Teaching swimming is not just about learning a series of movements. It also has to do with instincts and attitude. When the mind is afraid and insecure, invariably, movement suffers. The teacher/swimmer, then, must go beyond the movement. *The teacher swimmer must focus on the mental process as it impacts movement itself.*

But how do you measure mental process? A strategy is to measure a learner's growth incrementally, always asking the question: **"What is the most important need of the learner right now?"** How do you discover this need? You discover it by carefully studying the learner and tuning in to all of the little changes and nuances during each session in the water; searching for all the little tell-tale signs by which the learner reveals the inner-self; learning to concentrate on these tell-tale signs and seeking solutions which go beyond the **obvious**.

THE RIGHT FIELDER

When he was eight years old, my oldest son, Matt, played on a Little League baseball team. The right fielder on his team was fast, a good hitter and fielder, but his ability to throw the ball with power left much to be desired. Each time he threw the ball for distance it ended up dramatically under thrown. The tell-tale look of frustration and embarrassment was written all over the young boy's face.

One day while watching the team practice, my attention turned to the right fielder who was returning balls that were being hit to the outfield. I watched him throw over and over again. I recognized that something did not look right, but could not pinpoint what it was. Finally, it hit me. The boy was throwing with his right arm and stepping forward with his right foot, instead of his left foot. I took him aside and suggested the change. He immediately doubled his distance on the next throw.

Generally speaking, most people instinctively step with the opposite foot when they throw. The body has a marvelous way of figuring these things out. *Obviously*, the answer to improving your distance when you throw is to "practice." But in this case, the solution went beyond the *obvious*. The tell-tale sign was: "something just does not look right."

BODY SURFING

As a young boy, I loved to body surf in the ocean. I would position myself in the water at a depth about waist high, waiting for a wave to come in and "break" toward the shore. As a breaking wave approached me, I would take a breath and dive face down with the wave towards the beach with my arms and legs extended, riding the wave as far as it would take me. At the end of my ride I would immediately jump up, turn around and work my way back to where the waves were breaking. Each time I anxiously anticipated the next ride. I would do this over and over again for hours.

Suddenly, and without warning, I would find myself with a mouthful of sea water. My wind pipe was totally clogged. I experienced a feeling of sheer utter horror. I could not breathe. I gasped and sputtered for air. Eventually, I was able to catch my breath and the feeling of horror passed.

I realized that each time I would finish my ride on the wave, I enthusiastically jumped up and immediately turned around for the next ride. Usually this did not present a problem. But occasionally, a powerful wave, breaking at the point where I turned around, would catch me completely off-guard. Result? I ended up with a mouthful of water, often being knocked down.

Naturally, I decided to pay better attention at the end of the ride. I had just experientially learned the hard way that you cannot predict wave patterns with absolute certainty. For a while, thereafter, I would become extremely cautious. The experience was vividly etched in my mind. But time has a funny way of making you forget when you are young. I would inevitably let my guard down and ended up once again with a mouthful of water. I found myself making the same mistake over and over again.

It was not until years later that I discovered that my assessment of being careful of an unexpected wave was only a half-truth. There was a second very important dynamic simultaneously occurring each time I rode a wave. When I turned around at the end of my ride, I was also taking a breath. I greeted the unexpected wave with my mouth wide open. During the ride, I was holding my breath. At the end of my ride, I instinctively took a breath. My actions were always the same. I would exhale, turn around and if the conditions were right, bingo, I ended up sucking in a mouthful of water.

Not only should I have been paying attention to the unexpected wave, I should also have been learning to keep my mouth shut. The answer to my dilemma went beyond the _obvious_.

If I were predisposed to give up, I would have stopped body surfing altogether because of my inability to control an unexpected wave. *Obviously*, you can never control the occurrence of an unexpected wave. On the other hand, you can certainly learn to keep your mouth shut! Learning to keep my mouth shut was a milestone in the formulation of my own personal mind-body connection. Never again did I end up with a mouthful of water when body surfing!

FEAR

A DROWNING SCENARIO

"I am standing by the edge of the pool. All of a sudden I am falling - falling into the water. I reach out to break the fall. I hit the water. My body is on top of the water. What is happening? Some water went up my nose. My eyes are not seeing like they normally do. I dare not rub them. I am so confused and disoriented. I feel out of con-

trol. I lift my head as high and back as possible trying to catch a breath. I reach and grab at the water to my sides and try to push my head above water to breathe. But the water cannot always lift me. I am sinking. I cannot touch the bottom. I need some air but I cannot catch a breath. The horror, I am going to drown."

Fear of drowning is a rational fear and is no different from the fear of heights or fire. Fear protects us. Fear is healthy and is our reality check. On occasion, I go up on a ladder to inspect the roof of my house. Each time I get on a ladder, I find myself carefully measuring each step from rung to rung. I am not thinking about anything else. I am not fluid in my movements. It is not like climbing a flight of stairs where my mind and body are totally in synch. When I step from the ladder on to the roof, I realize that I am now even more vulnerable to falling. I take a deep breath to relieve the anxiety. At this point I would rather stay on the ladder. Actually, I look for excuses not to climb on the roof.

Roofers on the other hand go up and down ladders all the time. They don't hesitate to climb on a roof. They have experience. They climb on a roof so often that it is second nature to them. They are fluid in their movements. Their mind and body are totally in synch. There is always a danger of falling but the danger is offset by confidence. The confidence comes from competence and the competence comes from knowledge and experience.

Fear becomes unhealthy when it evolves into an irrational fear. When fear causes us to overreact to a situation or immobilizes us to the point of inaction, it is clearly dangerous to our well-being. It can be said that it is a rational decision when someone avoids certain situations because of an irrational fear. For instance, if you climb on a ladder and begin to panic, then you should stay off the ladder. This is only a matter of common sense.

There is one other consideration however. Suppose

there was a fire and you had to climb on a ladder to escape. How might you respond to this emergency? Would you panic and freeze - immobilized by the fear? Or, would you get on the ladder and climb to safety? Fear has thresholds and continuums. The way one would respond to a crisis situation differs from individual to individual and from circumstance to circumstance. Should we wait for a fire to find out how we would react in a fire? Maybe one would be better advised to develop a fire escape plan and preemptively deal with the problem.

The point I am trying to make is that we can compensate for and minimize danger by developing life skills experiences and strategies.. Sometimes it makes more sense to walk around a fence rather than trying to jump over it. The same holds true for swimming. Instead of trying to take on our fear "head-on" (the old "sink or swim" approach), it is better to develop skills and experiences that build up our confidence. This in turn raises our risk-taking threshold. Keep on chipping away until you master the fear. **Recognizing each element of your fear and dealing with it in a safe, supervised, non-threatening environment bridges the gap separating the mind from the body.**

ORIGINS OF FEAR

BODIES OF WATER ARE MYSTERIOUS

As a young boy I had a fantasy about what it would be like if all the water behind my home went out to sea for a day, a low tide that went on for miles and miles revealing a bottom which had always been hidden from my view. I would see sunken ships. Islands would become mountains. Boats would be sitting in the mud with their anchors and chains exposed. I would walk along the bottom exploring all of the wonders which up until this time had been masked by the water. Mysteries would become unfolded right before my very eyes.

Water is always level. There are no mountains and valleys. We can see for miles along the top of water straight into the horizon. Our ability to see what is below the water is measured in terms of feet and inches. **The element of lurking dangers under the water real or imagined is always present.**

Pools, lakes, rivers and oceans are not bathtubs where you are caressed on the bottom and sides. The expansiveness of bodies of water is exhilarating to some, frightening to others. **The element that connects both the exhilaration and the fear is vulnerability.** It appears that this feeling is a pervasive feeling among most people – swimmer and non-swimmer alike.

Each person has risk thresholds, skills, and experiences that impact his/her sense of security in the water. Once again, you are talking about a continuum. A person who has no fear of water in a pool, may, on the other hand, be totally intimidated by oceans and rivers. As a matter of fact, it is quite prudent if you have limited or no water experience outside of a pool to proceed warily into oceans, rivers or any unfamiliar body of water.

Lack of water clarity and swimming in the dark further contribute to these feelings of vulnerability. Who can forget the opening scene of the movie "Jaws" which will forever change swimming habits of people at night.

WATER ANOMALIES

It has always amazed me how people who are quite proficient in the water in so many ways claim that they are afraid of the water. People who are senior lifesavers, scuba divers etc. very often make this claim.

A number of years ago, a group of us asked a local owner of a small sailboat to take us to a small island off Fajardo in Puerto Rico. It was our first day of vacation during our first winter break. I was ecstatic just to be there and felt intoxicated by the beauty and warmth of my surroundings. The group included my son, Eric, his friend Michael, both 15, my wife, Barbara, and our dear friend, Bernadette, who for many years was my wife's employer and mentor.

We anchored about 50 yards off-shore. I jumped into the water and began to swim toward the small island. Eric and Michael jumped in right after me and we swam to the island delirious with joy. My wife and Bernadette did not share our delirium, however, since they were somewhat intimidated by going into the water 50 yards off shore from the island. We were in open water, a number of miles from the Puerto Rican mainland. They thought that they could be swept away in a current and they let me know about it in no uncertain terms.

It was their opinion that I should have remained there to make sure that they were safe. They were right! Both Barbara and Bernadette are accomplished swimmers. It never dawned on me that they would feel this way since I knew experientially that there was no danger. The problem was that they did not realize that there was no danger.

I was quite embarrassed by my insensitivity. It was bad enough that I was insensitive but it was also the first day that we were vacationing with my wife's boss of 8 years. Talk about first impressions! It was, however, a learning experience for me. I will never make that mistake again!

CHOKING

The experience of getting water in your nose is quite unpleasant and very often leads to choking. The same can be said of water entering through your mouth. Water getting in your windpipe inadvertently, causing you to gag, can be very uncomfortable as well as frightening. It is easy to understand why learners would be apprehensive about putting their heads in the water if they felt there was a risk of choking. Learners are apprehensive since they cannot, with certainty, be absolutely sure that they can control the water from entering the windpipe through the mouth and nose. **The learner never experienced this control.** Suffocation, one could say, is fear of choking in its most extreme form.

LOSS OF CONTROL

Fear of **letting go**, loss of control and the feeling of being disoriented is a very real stumbling block in learning how to swim. Except for swimming, I cannot think of any experience when at least some part of the body is not oriented to something solid. When we stand, walk and run we are oriented to the ground by our feet. When we recline, our body is oriented to whatever it is we are lying on. When we sit, our body is oriented to whatever it is we are sitting on. **At all times we are touching something solid.**

Water on the other hand is a liquid. It is quite understandable why many learners find it difficult to let go. They will not be touching something solid for the first time in their entire lives. *They are suspended in a liquid medium.* It is a feeling that one can relate to by experience only. Once again we are dealing with a risk taking continuum. The willingness to **let go** varies from individual to individual.

One of my favorite analogies is for those who have ever tried to teach a child to ride a bicycle. Telling a learner to pedal harder when losing one's balance seems so incongruous, when the instinct is to stop altogether in order not to fall. The learner must experience the feeling of balance, control and stability before gaining the confidence needed to pedal harder in order to keep a bicycle stabilized. The only way to gain this experience is by taking a risk. Taking a risk involves both facing and trying to overcome one's fears.

Letting go and surrendering to the experience of disorientation is probably the most pervasive stumbling

block to learning how to swim. It has been my experience that it is much easier to get the learner to put the head in the water especially when wearing a mask or goggles. However, the willingness to **let go** is an internal decision that the learner must make on his/her own. Eventually, a learner will do it. It is just a question of time. **Let us not forget that the level of trust the learner has in the teacher/swimmer accelerates the process.**

OPENING THE EYES

Fear of opening the eyes underwater goes hand in hand with the feeling of **letting go**. Just imagine closing your eyes in an unfamiliar medium (water) and letting go for the first time. **It is easy to see why closing the eyes while suspended in water can bring about a feeling of disorientation and lack of control.** How do you keep your balance? **How do you recover?** Sure, it is easy to say there is nothing to it. But is that true? Only experience can truly alleviate the fears of opening the eyes, loss of control, and disorientation. But, you must trust and take a risk to gain the experience to alleviate fear. Once again, we are talking about thresholds and continuums.

An interesting aside on the subject of opening your eyes underwater is the reaction of some experienced swimmers who are involved in scuba training. One of the skills required is removing a mask underwater and putting it back on. This is executed while the student is breathing air through the aqualung apparatus called a "regulator." Sounds simple enough, but some students are so insecure in executing this maneuver that they cannot comfortably breathe through a mouthpiece with blurred vision. They feel much too disoriented and out of control. There is no real danger, but the feeling of blurred vision underwater and breathing through a mouthpiece at the same time intimidates students almost to the point of panic. Mind and body refuse to connect.

EMBARRASSMENT

Fear of embarrassment is another factor with which the learner has to contend. The learner may feel embarrassed about his/her body. The learner may be embarrassed by the fear. The learner may be afraid of looking foolish. The learner may be afraid of being teased. The list can go on and on. **Negative experiences will simply reinforce these fears.**

TRAUMA

Many non-swimmers have been traumatized by some kind of frightening experience while in a water environment. Trauma leaves the victim with indelible scars on the psyche. Some learners have been insensitively pushed or thrown into water. Others have been "ducked" and held under the water, rendered powerless under the guise of "having fun." (It has always amazed me how some people tease others to the point of mental torture and call it having "fun.") **It really does not matter how much real danger is involved. It is the perception of danger that causes the trauma.** It is how the psyche processes the frightening experience that determines the level or degree of trauma.

POST TRAUMA

The damage to the psyche can get worse over time. A child looking for sympathy and attention will tell a frightened parent how he/she "almost drowned" and at the same time embellish the incident to the point where fact and fiction become clouded. It is similar to the phenomenon where people sue for a bogus "whiplash" and convince themselves that they really have a neck injury. In time, they end up with all the symptoms of neck injury.

REACT

It is imperative for those entrusted with the well-being of a traumatized learner to deal with the frightening incident immediately. Never let the trauma process get into gear if possible. Nip it in the bud! Always be sensitive to the feelings of the learner or else you may unwittingly allow the trauma process to take hold. **Keep in mind that the perception of danger is more important than the danger itself.** Very often sensitivity, caring and understanding can work miracles. Be a good listener! Study facial expressions and body language. Look in the victim's eyes. Take charge and never ignore the trauma no matter how insignificant it may seem.

INFANCY

It is my belief that much of the fear of water begins very early in life. Just imagine for a moment how many new experiences new born children encounter each day. They must learn how to take liquids into their body. If they are not held correctly they very often choke on their formula. The nipple in the bottle may get clogged. They may drink too fast. They suffer from gas pains. If they are breast fed the mother may not be producing enough milk. They must be bathed. They are totally dependent upon their parents for their comfort and sustenance.

Now think for a moment about the mental state of the parents. Raising a baby can be a totally new experience. The baby's neck is very fragile. Some babies cry so hard that they may stop breathing and pass out. They can choke on their bottle in the crib. The amount of responsibility can be mind boggling.

Let us consider for a moment what is involved in bathing a child. We cannot allow the child to slip out of our hands. We must protect the child's neck. We do not want the child to swallow and choke on the water. We do not want to get soap in the child's eyes. We must wash the child's hair and scalp. We hold the child very tightly. The child may be cold. We do not want the child to get sick. Crying is the child's only form of protest. The child can sense our nervousness. Tension! Tension! Tension!

Is it possible that it is the bathing experience which initiates fear of water? Once again we are talking about thresholds and continuums. We are also talking about the fears, experiences, temperament and attitudes of the person bathing the child.

Let us try to envision how the child is instinctively processing the bathing experience. Let us try to place ourselves in the mind of the child.

"I can feel the tension in the parent bathing me."

"Something is different."

"I do not feel secure."

"The parent who I am totally dependent upon and trust seems scared."

"Things are happening so fast."

"I cry in protest but water went into my mouth and nose."

"My parent is not trying to please me."

"My parent pushes my head back and pours water over my scalp."

"My parent seems so upset."

"I do not like what is happening to me."

Now suppose the child, for whatever reason, slips out of the parent's arms and briefly goes under the water. What if the parent has deep rooted fear of the water? The child, remember, is stunned and cannot process what has happened. The parent quickly grabs the child to make sure the child is still breathing. The child opens its eyes and the first thing it sees is the look of horror on the parent's face. Has this child been traumatized? I suspect it has. It is not the incident alone that caused the trauma. Rather, it was the reaction of the well-meaning parent. Many eating disorders are blamed on the attitudes of parents. Many psychological problems are blamed on toilet training. **Could it be that fear of the water originates with bathing?**

FOOD FOR THOUGHT

The following is quoted from Herman Melville's *Typee*:

"One day, in company with Kory-Kory, I had repaired to the stream for the purpose of bathing , when I observed a woman sitting upon a rock in the midst of the current, and watching with the liveliest interest the gambols of something, which at first I took to be an uncommonly large species of frog that was sporting in the water near her. Attracted by the novelty of the sight, I waded towards the spot where she sat, and could hardly credit the evidence of my senses when I beheld a little infant, the period of whose birth could not have extended back many days, paddling about as if it had just risen to the surface, after being hatched into existence at the bottom. Occasionally the delighted parent reached out her hand towards it, when the little thing, uttering a faint cry, and striking out its tiny limbs, would sidle for the rock, and the next moment be clasped to its mother's bosom. This was repeated again and again, the baby remaining in the stream about a minute at a time. Once or twice it made wry faces at swallowing a mouthful of water, and choked and spluttered as if on the point of strangling. At such times, however the mother snatched it up, and by a process scarcely to be mentioned, obliged it to eject the fluid. For several weeks afterward, I observed the woman bringing her down to the stream regularly every day, in the cool of the morning and evening, and treating it to a bath. No wonder that the South Seas islanders are so amphibious a race when they are thus launched into the water as soon as they see the light. I am convinced that it is as natural for a human being to swim as it is for the duck. And yet, in civilized communities, how many able-bodied individuals die, like

so many drowning kittens from the occurrence of the most trivial accident!"

FEAR REINFORCED

Fear of the water can be reinforced as the child grows older with such insensitive phrases such as: "Don't go near the water, you are going to drown."

Just think about that expression for a moment. You are telling the child that if the child goes near the water the child is going to die. Scary, isn't it? How many irrational fears end up in a child's subconscious mind because of the unintentional insensitivity of adults.

Just this past summer, a friend of mine was telling me how upset he was listening to a mother tell her small boy not to go too far into the water because the sea monster was going to get him. The parent's heart might be in the right place since the parent honestly thinks that she is protecting her child. Unfortunately, the parent has no idea about the kind of psychological damage such an expression can cause the child. As the child matures, the child will realize that there are no sea monsters to get him. But how does he remove the fear that was impressed into his subconscious mind? The worst part of all is that these kind of insensitive phrases perpetuate themselves from generation to generation.

OTHER

The mind can conjure up its own fears. As a young boy, I had a fear that probably was uniquely mine. I was known as the "clamdigger." I would sell clams at 30 cents a dozen to a group of regular customers who were always in need of my services. To off-islanders (usually boat owners), I was the "kid" and they always came looking for me when they wanted some clams to eat.

My method was quite simple. I would take a deep

breath, dive underwater with a mask and fins, look for the clam holes and dig. I would grab anywhere from 3-6 clams and swim to the surface totally out of breath. I would swim to a wooden fruit basket inside an automobile inner tube and drop the clams inside the basket. I would then swim to an area where the bottom was not stirred up and start all over again.

I developed a tremendous breath since I would keep digging until my lungs were ready to burst. I did this over and over again. But what would happen if I got my finger stuck in a chain link on the murky bottom as I was digging? If it was toward the end of my breath, I would suffocate. Coincidentally, the area where I dug for clams was also a mooring area. Boats were held in place with heavy chains and anchors. The probability of getting my finger stuck in a chain link was quite remote. However, whenever I felt a heavy chain while digging for clams, I would shudder.

THE PANIC RESPONSE

One time while working as a lifeguard at Orchard Beach, I was watching a young man holding a young woman with one arm under her shoulders and the other arm under her knees supported by the buoyancy of the water. The young woman held her arms tenderly around the young man's neck. Let's call them Joe and Nancy. Moving along in chest high water, they were totally engrossed in each other but were perilously close to one of the abrupt "drops"-a sudden change in the depth of the water occurring at low tide.

Joe suddenly and unexpectedly stepped off one of the "drops." The couple were, without warning, over their heads. Nancy clung to Joe's neck for dear life. Bottom line? They were drowning!

Joe made a feeble attempt to save her but quickly gave up. He swam in 5-6 feet to where he could stand, leaving Nancy alone drowning by herself. There was a look of absolute terror in the poor girl's eyes. Joe did not say or do anything. He just stood there watching her with his hands on his hips. I immediately ran into the water and saved her. As I brought Nancy to safety, Joe approached her to console her. I believe that, as far as she was concerned, the relationship was over. Joe was no knight in shining armor. *If looks could kill!*

This situation demonstrates the two extremes of the panic response. Nancy over-reacted; Joe under-reacted. She was in a total state of panic. He froze. Joe never even thought of calling for help or giving some words of encouragement to the drowning young woman. He did nothing. The truth is that minimal skills were required on both their parts to bring the situation under control. If I were not there, chances are that Nancy would have drowned. She was totally incapable of saving herself.

Experiences such as the one above molded in my mind what later became the basic premise of my attitude toward teaching swimming at PS32 – SURVIVAL.

In retrospect, if I were Nancy's teacher, the first thing I would do is gently smile and acknowledge the fact that she was really scared. If Nancy also smiles, I have just overcome the first hurdle in diffusing the fear process. I would explain to her that she did not drown but was in a drowning situation. There is a difference. The fact that I was there to save her removes any real element of danger. That's my job. There is no real correlation between being scared and danger. **The feeling of being scared is how the mind processes a situation. The degree of danger depends upon the situation itself.**

The discussion would now move to what are some of the strategies we can use when we find ourselves over our heads and unable to touch bottom. I would ask her to demonstrate some of these skills in shallow water. In some cases, if I felt the student was capable enough (and willing enough), we would go back to the deep end and recreate the drowning experience. **(Swimming in deep water for the first time is a big psychological hurdle for most swimmers, whether or not they had a drowning experience.)**

My reaction as a teacher/swimmer is critical. If I were to berate her about how irresponsible she was for going in over her head, for whose emotional benefit would I be doing it? Hers? or Mine? Acting like it did not happen, does not negate the experience. It happened! *The incident demands intervention.* **At this point you are suddenly lifted to a position of incredible power and responsibility.** This young lady could be emotionally scarred for life if you do not address the problem with sensitivity and understanding.

The physical safety of any person left in your charge is always the number one responsibility of a teacher/swimmer. This is immutable. The ability to adapt and react to the constantly changing needs of the learner follows safety. **An emotional event such as a perceived near drowning experience demands a re-prioritization of our teaching goals immediately.** It does not matter what is the true level of danger; it is the perception of danger in the mind of the learner that counts. Sensitivity to these feelings are imperative to becoming an effective teacher/swimmer.

One time I heard the expression: " Teacher, teacher the bird just died and you kept on talking." It may have been the name of a book or a segment in a book. The point I am trying to make is that our focus must change as circumstances change. The needs of a learner and the plans of a teacher are not always in synch.

WATER TEMPERATURE

There is a direct correlation between the progress of the learner and the learning environment. It is the job of the teacher/swimmer to try and understand the various forces that impact a learning environment and control them.

One of my pet peeves is water temperature. It has been my experience that the water temperature in many municipal swimming pool environments is rather cool. Private institutions seem to do a much better job at climate control than the public sector. I have yet to go to an indoor hotel pool or indoor health club pool where the water temperature was uncomfortable.

CATCH 22

The reason I mention this fact is that I believe many people never bothered to learn how to swim because they have been turned off by the discomfort of the water temperature among other things. Why would anybody want to place themselves in cold water unless they are pre-disposed to enjoy cold water? **If you know how to swim, the exertion involved in swimming will raise your body temperature to a comfortable level.** *But if you cannot swim, how do you raise your body temperature? There is no way of getting warm.* The discomfort involved in learning how to swim under these circumstances is just not worth it. It is too uncomfortable. Why bother? *Compounding the problem is the fact that there is usually no compelling need in the eyes of the young learner to learn how to swim in the first place.* The situation becomes a real catch-22.

I believe that the current fitness trends are doing wonders for the absolute necessity of a comfortable swimming environment. Older adults, especially senior citizens, are swimming more. They insist on being comfortable since they are swimming for pleasure and fitness. Cold water is unacceptable. They know better. They demand better.

Historically, the public sector is not as accountable as the private sector. The public sector can dazzle you with reasons, excuses, policy and someone to blame. It is much too easy to pass the buck. The private sector, on the other hand, is held much more accountable since their funding is fee based. If they are not responsive to the comfort level of their clients, they will lose business. Eventually, they will be out of business. The public sector too often responds only to rallies, protests, notoriety and political pressure. This is not to say that everyone working in the public sector is uncaring, but the problem is systemic.

Just imagine for a moment that you own a car. But this car has some little idiosyncrasies. It doesn't start in wet weather. It does not like cold days. It is always breaking down. Why deal with the frustration? Perhaps you're better off taking the bus! Applying the same reasoning to a swimming pool, how many learners have been subtly turned off to learning how to swim because of an uncomfortable or unreliable swimming environment? We are not just talking about water temperature. Let's not forget when the showers run out of hot water and you end up walking away with a deathly chill.

THE "EYES" OF THE LEARNER

Let's look at the process. The learner is young. The learner is afraid. The preposterousness of asking a non-swimmer to learn to swim in an uncomfortable environment never occurs to the learner. The beginner accepts this since he/she does not know any better and does not have a point of reference for comparison. The learner concludes, "I don't like to swim because the water is too cold!"

Consequently, the feeling of discomfort causes the learner to look for excuses to avoid the situation altogether and drop out. The end result is that the learner never learns to swim, will never be water-safe, and is being shut out from participating in a pleasurable lifestyle.

When my youngest son Eric was 5 years old, I took him for swimming lessons geared toward his age group at a local high school. The classes were held on Saturday morning. It was wintertime and the place was downright cold. The pool, the deck, the locker rooms, the water. Everything! To top it all off, the showers ran out of hot water. This program should have been called: *"Teaching Young Masochists How To Swim"*! There were always apologies and excuses. Meanwhile, I was busy trying to share a wonderful bonding experience with my son.

Fortunately, my son is a water person. He did not like swimming in this place. Neither did I! Fortunately, this experience did not tarnish his joy of swimming in other places. He knew the difference. Upon reflection, what about the children who were less fortunate in terms of water experiences? How are they doing today?

WARM / COLD PEOPLE

There are those of us who tend to be "warm" people and those of us who are "cold" people. What I mean is this: some people tend to be warm all the time and some people tend to be cold all of the time. Usually, cold people enjoy the invigorating coolness of water; warm people enjoy the caressing warmth. The best compromise is a steady water temperature of 82° – 85°.

COMFORT ZONES

We all have comfort zones. The comfort zones are the places where we feel safe physically, psychologically, emotionally and spiritually. Venturing out of our comfort zones involves risk. Let us look into the mind of the child:

"The pool is big and scary."

"I feel embarrassed wearing a bathing suit, especially among my friends."

"I hope they do not laugh at me."

"I hope nobody teases me about my body."

"What if water goes up my nose and in my mouth causing me to choke?"

"I hope nobody grabs me or splashes me."

"What if the teacher asks me to put my head in the water?"

"What if I should look foolish if the teacher calls on me?"

"What if the other children realize how scared I really am?"

"I am so nervous about being here!".

POSITIVE EXPERIENCE

Learning to swim should be a positive experience. Positive experiences draw people out of their comfort zones. Positive experiences are motivators which give the learner the self-confidence to take risks. *Positive experiences give the mind the ability to trust the body.*

ADULTS: *LISTEN-UP!*

Let us remember that we were all children at one time. Childhood was a time when we, for the most part, accepted our experiences without questioning. These experiences laid the groundwork for many of our fears, attitudes and even our abilities. As you read, I hope little bells are going off and you are beginning to focus on the basically **external** causes of water related attitudes and feelings which are later internalized by the individual. I am trying to uncover the common threads that can assist us as parents, teachers or someone just interested in self-help.

BAGGAGE

Most people whom I have encountered are predisposed to enjoy the water. The level of predisposition to enjoy the water is modified by other factors that I like to call **"baggage"** – fear, vanity, modesty, impatience, laziness, negative feelings, insensitive experiences and trauma, to name a few. *Children who by nature are more spontaneous and* *less complicated than adults are highly predisposed to enjoy the water.* They are much more receptive to new ideas and experiences. Keeping this in mind, teaching someone to swim is not terribly complicated, provided that it is a positive experience for the learner. *A positive experience is the best antidote to dealing with any "baggage."*

SUPPORTS

Just as some learners come to a water environment with *"baggage,"* some learners come to a water environment with *"supports."* The learner may be well coordinated. The learner may feel extremely good about himself/herself. The learner may have involved parents who take tremendous pleasure in sharing in the learner's growth and success. The learner may have a lifestyle that is conducive to learning how to swim.

MIKIE

Each year my wife and I visit with our dear friends, Peter and Bernadette, in Puerto Rico during February break. (In case you were wondering, it is the same Bernadette that I *unimpressed* years earlier.) Both Peter and Bernadette are retired educators who have profoundly influenced both my wife and myself in terms of professional development. We regard both Peter and Bernadette as true leaders in the field of education.

Peter and Bernadette have a son, Michael, who is hearing impaired. Michael is married to Suzann, who is also hearing impaired. They have a wonderful six year old son, "Mikie," who is not hearing impaired. Coincidentally, we were all vacationing at the same time. Bernadette felt that if Mikie were alone and fell into the water, his parents would not be able hear him if he called for help. It was time for Mikie to learn how to swim. The responsibility was uniquely mine.

I had some reservations. Mikie was a little younger than the children I was used to teaching. This was the first time my teaching style and techniques would come under the careful scrutiny of such outstanding educators. My mission had to be accomplished in seven days.

The air was warm. The water was warm. We all spent the entire afternoon lounging around the pool. Mikie's dad was a competitive swimmer – very accomplished – much more skilled than myself. Mikie was motivated. His family was totally supportive. Nobody interfered with my teaching. I was given a free rein.

Mikie had some of the typical fears. He did not, at first, want to put his head in the water. He did not want to **let go**. These type of reactions are to be expected. He obviously was never traumatized.

Mikie was smart. He was coordinated. He was trusting. He was happy. His family were water people. There was a very special bond with his parents that was a pleasure to watch. Six days later Mikie was snorkeling over his head 50 yards off-shore with his parents as if it were second nature. Mission accomplished! (As an aside, Mikie and his parents have a special skill in comparison to the average group of snorkelers. They can communicate with each other underwater using sign language.)

This experience was very gratifying for me as well. The process of teaching Mikie to swim was fun, especially in such a comfortable environment. I enjoyed discussing Mikie's progress with Peter and Bernadette because their opinions (and approval) were important to me. My teaching methods were validated. I experienced what I consider the ultimate teacher/swimmer *"rush."* That is, I taught and witnessed a learner swimming with competence for the first time as a result of my efforts. It is a feeling of which you never tire. It gives you a sense of personal satisfaction and accomplishment.

SUMMARY

One can readily assume that a learner may have any number of attitudes, feelings and fears in varying degrees. Each learner must be seen as an individual with unique needs, tolerances, fears and experiences. The biggest mistake a person entrusted with the responsibility of teaching someone to become water competent is to assume too much or too little. *An approach to teaching that does not allow for individual differences is fatally flawed.* Even worse is when we try to project our own feelings and attitudes upon the learner. Empathize with the learner in a non-judgmental way and the pieces of the puzzle will fall into place. The mind and body eventually will connect.

3
WATERSAFE PROGRAM

What should be our goals? What should be our objectives? What is it we are really trying to accomplish when we teach water competence? As teacher/swimmers, we should set goals and in many cases have dreams for those left in our charge. The question which first must be answered before all other questions is: **"What is the minimum standard of water competence we are trying to achieve"?**

The above point is critical since many factors, personal and universal, affect each individual's necessary standard of water competence. For instance, if you live near the ocean, there is an immediate need for the learner to become a strong swimmer. Winds, currents, undertows, rip tides etc. demand a high level of swimming ability. If the only swimming you will do is at the local swimming pool, the level of skill necessary to keep one water-safe is much less. The issue becomes: "What is the minimum level of competence necessary to make the learner water-safe in the learner's **routine** swimming environment"? *Safety* **is the key universal factor that dictates the correct level of minimum competence for all swimming environments.** How skillful the learner must become in order to achieve a minimum level of water competence and at the same time assure the learner's safety is dictated by the swimming environment itself.

ASSESSMENT

The ability to be water-safe in and around water is a necessary life skill. The level of skill necessary to be water-safe, however, varies from circumstance to circumstance. In addition, an individual may have needs that will not be met merely by achieving minimal competence. For these people, swimming can be a recreational skill – a competitive skill – a fitness skill – a job-related skill – a social skill, or any combination of the above. Therefore, we must do an assessment. We must assess the attitudes, needs, priorities, capabilities, lifestyle and experiences as they pertain to the necessary level of water competence we need to achieve. Our level of water mastery should uniquely reflect the needs established in this assessment. In other words, **let's be realistic**. Where does swimming fit into a learner's lifestyle? Which water-safe skills are necessary for the learner to master at a given point in time in order to be safe in and near the water?

Say, for instance, your family belongs to a recreational club with a pool and tennis courts. Let us assume that from the minute your child gets to the club, he/she goes immediately to the tennis courts and is content to play there all day long. Perhaps at the end of the day, your child likes to take a "dip" in the pool in order to cool off. Rest assured, it does not take many skills to water-safe this child. The level of skill necessary to protect this youngster under these circumstances is minimal. The child will probably learn how to swim simply by watching the other swimmers, copying their movements.

But if your child becomes friends with his/her peers around the pool, learning becomes a "fait accompli." Swimming under these circumstances is a comfortable, playful experience. Why *not* learn how to swim ? **Swimming is fun!** Learning to swim affords the child more ways to socialize and enjoy water-related activities; an immediate need to learn how to swim has been created. *This need to learn to swim is internal.* This internal need results in the child becoming motivated. This motivation, as it turns out, is the best motivation of all – *self-motivation!*

TIMING

By introducing some non-threatening swimming tips at this time leads to, in most cases, unbelievable progress. Avoid the inclination to be too overbearing. It's all about timing and presentation. Never separate the skill from the strategy. Never sacrifice the process for the product. Think long range. Rest assured this child is motivated. Make it fun and the child will learn how to swim.

Sometimes doing nothing and just observing the learner is the best strategy of all. Yogi Berra, the great New York Yankeee catcher, once said, **"Sometimes you can observe a whole lot by just watching."**

You cannot simply tell a learner to forget about the fears that impact his/her attitude toward water at a given point in time. You cannot always convince the learner that it is even necessary to learn how to swim. The learner may be quite content to remain entrenched in the comfort zones.

What to do? Be patient! The key to facilitating the mind-body connection is to enrich the positive water experiences of the learner. Keep on chipping away with positive experiences and the fears will soon pass on their own. Raise that beginner's level of awareness and the learner will soon realize there was nothing to fear but the fears themselves. The **internal** need to learn how to swim has now been established. The mind and body are in the process of connecting.

TRUST

Teacher/swimmer attitude is critical in dealing with the beginning swimmer. Essentially, the teacher/swimmer must always be monitoring the mind-body connection. Learners should always be encouraged to leave their comfort zones. If the teacher/swimmer carefully plans, the learner should instinctively know that the swimming environment is safe, supervised, and non-threatening. This knowledge gives the learner the necessary confidence to actually leave the comfort zone.

The sense of security that the learner should feel in a swimming environment is similar to riding on a roller coaster. The rider may feel frightened but at the same time feels safe because he/she implicitly trusts the operator for safety and protection. **The key word here is _trust_.** While the rider experientially feels a sense of danger, the mind assures that the experience is safe. This sense of security and trust enables the rider to take risks. The rider is now motivated to leave his/her comfort zone. Each subsequent ride further verifies this trust and the fear soon dissipates. The rider laughs and enjoys the thrill, and as a result now welcomes the next challenge.

ATTITUDE

What should be the components of teacher/swimmer attitude? To begin with the teacher/swimmer should exude the feeling that just being in and around the water is fun. A smiling happy teacher/swimmer creates a contagion of positive energy. "Grumps" and people who take themselves too seriously need not apply!

Secondly, the swimming environment must be safe and the learner must implicitly sense that he/she is in a safe environment.

Once the safety parameters are in place, I like to use the "*No Big Deal*" approach. For example: you slip and fall down. Does this mean that you are some kind of a "klutz?" Obviously not! You simply slipped and fell down. If someone laughs at you, the *mind* tells you to be embarrassed. If someone tells you that you always are falling down, the *mind* begins to make you feel that you are clumsy. If someone hysterically asks you if you are "OK," the *mind* tells you that you escaped some kind of imminent danger. If someone gently smiles and asks you how you are doing, your *mind* is put at ease.

Your *mind* should be free to make its own assessment of the situation when you fall. Chances are that you simply fell down. But you should be free to make this decision without any "baggage" imposed on you from the outside. This approach, although quite subtle, is critical to facilitating the mind-body connection.

A person who truly cares will be a support. A person who cares will empathize with you, will listen and laugh with you – not at you. This person may embellish the incident by telling you how he/she fell under similar circumstances. This friend will put you at ease, making you feel that what happened to you was "*No Big Deal*".

"HANDS-ON" vs. "HANDS-OFF"

A teacher/swimmer at times must be a virtual chameleon. There are situations when a teacher/swimmer's role must be **"hands-on."** And there are times when the role of a teacher/swimmer should be **"hands-off."** Depending upon the learning style of the learner, the teacher/swimmer must be able to recognize and be flexible enough to adapt to each learner's individual needs.

There are learners who are motivated by the interaction with the instructor. Bonding plays an integral role in their progress. These learners learn best when the teacher approach is **"hands-on."**

Other learners prefer to be left alone to practice on their own. These learners seek approval just like all other learners but do not necessarily need to bond with the teacher/swimmer. Generally speaking, they are somewhat shy and withdrawn. Interaction with the teacher/swimmer for these learners is more of a distraction rather than a benefit. They prefer to practice on their own and will let you know when they are in need of assistance. These learners will not necessarily tell you that they are in need of assistance but communicate via **"tell-tale"** signs. That is, their facial expression and body language tells you when to intervene and render assistance. The role of a teacher/swimmer for these learners is that of **"hands-off."** These learners are very often *"foolers."* They are the learners who do not seem to be paying attention but show up one day (especially after a summer vacation) replicating with considerable proficiency all of the skills that were taught in class.

FACILITATE

Whether the swimmer learns via **"hand's-on"** or **"hands-off,"** the primary role of the teacher/swimmer should be that of a *facilitator*. Learning how to swim is an **internal** process which varies from individual to individual. Each learner has his/her own learning style. Each learner is a unique mixture of positive and negative experiences. Each learner is a unique mixture of skills and capabilities. There is no one way to teach each individual. The message must always be a **"constant."** How we deliver that message, however, should always be a **"variable."**

A facilitator focuses on the learning environment. The program itself should stand on its own. There is no need to hover over and control the learner's progress at all times. The facilitator blends in with and does not dominate those left in his/her charge. The facilitator is the conductor that orchestrates a wonderful symphony that is unique for each individual.

FLEXIBILITY

A teacher/swimmer cannot always predict outcomes. Very often learners will discover certain movements on their own. A teacher/swimmer must be flexible enough to seize the moment and introduce skills and strategies out of what was a perceived sequence of skills to be taught.

Once I demonstrated the overhand arm stroke to a group of new fourth graders. Following the demonstration, a boy asked if he could demonstrate the stroke for the class. Naturally, I accommodated his request. He executed the stroke quite proficiently. I took him aside a short while after the lesson and asked him who taught him how to swim so well. Rarely could any of my new students swim. Swimming with proficiency and good form usually occurred only when a child moved to the city from the suburbs or some other non-urban environment. The boy told me that this was the first time he had ever been in a swimming pool. He had never been to a beach. He learned how to swim by watching the Summer Olympics on television the month before.

Interestingly enough, he was not a great athlete. In gym class, there was nothing about this boy to distinguish himself from the other children. Swimming for some reason came easy for this boy. His mind and body easily connected. His needs were very different than the needs of the other children. My teaching plan had to be modified to reflect those needs.

SAFETY

There are a number of considerations that must be taken into account before beginning a swimming lesson. The first consideration, as always, is safety. Watch out for broken glass and sharp objects. Broken glass can be a particularly difficult problem, especially around pools. Watch out for floatables. The same object that can hold you up can also carry you over your head. Make certain that you, the teacher/swimmer, has nothing to do that would cause you to leave your learner mentally or physically while at the swimming site. There is no substitute for direct supervision. It is not a good idea to get engrossed in your checkbook. It is not a good time to get something out of a closet. It is no time to daydream. Your learner must receive your undivided attention.

ZERO TOLERANCES

You, the teacher/swimmer, have been empowered with this tremendous opportunity to fundamentally change a learner's life forever. Never forget, your learner is quite vulnerable. **You have been entrusted with the physical, psychological, social, emotional and spiritual, yes, spiritual growth of this learner**. You can actually change this learner's fundamental mind-set about the water and, perhaps even more importantly, about trust forever. You can be the difference between whether this learner is water-safe or not water-safe. **Do not take your responsibilities lightly!**

It is the duty of the teacher/swimmer to command – to prepare – to laugh with the learner – to set the tone. Reckless behavior, rough-housing, teasing and insensitive laughter should never be tolerated. **Take charge!** Make sure that the swimming environment is sensitive, nurturing and caring. Encourage, and in some cases demand, that all members of your teaching environment be sensitive, nurturing and caring as well. **Lead by example**. Command and be sure to establish **zero tolerances** for any behavior that causes anyone left in your charge to suffer in any way.

4.
BUOYANCY AND PROPULSION

GRAVITY

If a person is in the water and remains motionless, the body will have a tendency to become vertical. The simple reason is that the lower body has a tendency to sink and the upper body has a tendency to float. The forces of gravity are at work in water just as they are on land. The earth has a tendency to pull you to it. A person who is sinking is really fighting the force of gravity, not the force of the water. Unlike on land, however, human beings cannot breathe under the water, which now makes the situation potentially life-threatening.

Movement on land allows you to move effortlessly horizontally with limited movement vertically. What I mean is that because of gravity, movement on land requires you to be anchored to something solid. The force of gravity does not allow for much vertical movement. If you jump, you can jump just so high and if you fall, you will keep on falling until you hit something solid.

Movement in water, on the other hand, is much different than movement on land. Floatation and propulsion ascent and descent requires the swimmer to utilize the viscosity (density) of water. The density or thickness of water resists movement. *It is this resistance to movement that is at the essence of our arm strokes and kicks.* Although this resistance, created by viscosity, does not allow the body to move as freely in water as it does on land, it allows the swimmer to propel the body through the water both horizontally and vertically. Water counteracts gravity by enabling a swimmer to resist it through movement.

RESISTANCE OF WATER

It is the resistance of water that enables the swimming arm strokes and kicks to elevate and propel the body. Resistance of water allows for a harmonious blending of the body and mind with the water. Learning to swim should not be viewed as a struggle with the water but rather as establishing a relationship with the water. **But, a relationship must be based upon understanding.** We must understand how water responds to our movements.

Due to fear and a lack of knowledge most beginning swimmers try to forcefully attack and overpower the water. For the most part, these efforts prove counterproductive. **Swimming is like dancing** – the more relaxed the body, the more fluid the movements. No pun intended. A relaxed body will maximize the resistance of water. The better approach then for the beginning swimmer is to develop a *"feel"* for the water. That is, learning how to flow with the water rather than trying to fight it. Body position in relation to the water impacts the effectiveness of the movement.

Kicking the legs brings the legs to the surface, stabilizes the body, and sometimes propels the body. Arm movements involve grabbing the water from the front of your body and pulling the water toward the back and sides of your body. For the most part, if force is exerted down, the body goes up. If force is exerted back, the body goes forward. Maximizing the resistance of water determines the effectiveness of the movement.

LEGS

Legs support your whole body. Just like a foundation holds up a building, legs hold up a person. Foundations are meant to support weight. They are heavy, strong, and dense. Legs are made out of muscle and bone. They too are heavy, strong, and dense. **An inactive leg will sink since it is too heavy to float.** Legs sink until your body is vertical in the water – straight up and down. **Legs literally pull the rest of the body under the water.**

The heaviness of the legs has far reaching implications for the drowning victim. In order to facilitate the mind-body connection, the drowning victim must realize that if the legs are allowed to sink, they will pull the victim under water as well as prevent forward movement.

Rule: **Get the legs moving! Don't let the legs sink.**

Use the resistance of the water to elevate and propel the legs. **Any rhythmic leg movement, such as simulated crawling, can be effective in producing resistance from the water, provided that the movement is rhythmic and causes the water to somehow resist it.**

Drowning victims forget to kick. They try to save themselves by using their arms only. **Water competency is in the legs.** It is the legs that pull the rest of the body under the water. _It is the legs that cause the body to sink._ In addition, you cannot **propel** the body with the legs extended too far under the water. There is too much _drag_. The body must be _streamlined_.

Streamlining is a critical concept. The closer the body becomes to being horizontal in the water the easier it is for the arms and legs to propel the body through the water or to just keep the body buoyant. Just think of how a boat moves. It must be on top of the water to make headway. My kick of choice for the beginning swimmer is the _"flutter"_ kick. The *flutter* kick can be used effectively with an arm in or arm out of the water arm stroke. The *flutter* kick can even be effective without any arm stroke, provided that the swimmer maintains a proper body alignment in the water. See section on the ***FLUTTER KICK.***

ARMS

An efficient rhythmic arm stroke is far more important than speed. It is how much water your arms and hands grab and hold on to that dictates the effectiveness of the arm stroke. **Speed follows form.** Just as in running, it is not the number of steps you take, it is the length of the stride. **The benefit of moving the arms fast is minimized if you are not grabbing and holding on to enough water.**

Very often we think of the function of the arms in the water only in terms of movement. Equally important is position. Extending the arms in front of the shoulders fosters not only **streamlining** but **counterbalancing** as well. By extending and pressing down on the water with the arms, the tendency of the legs to sink is **counterbalanced**. That is, the weight – position – and movement of the arms causes the legs to rise. Pulling back on the arms propels the body forward.

HEAD

Instinctively the fearful non-swimmer will try to lift the head as high as possible out of the water in order to breathe. Lifting the head as high as possible out of the water is a *counterproductive* movement. It **causes the legs to sink.** The key to proper head position is not lifting the head too high above the water, if at all. **Lowering the head fosters** *streamlining* **and** *counterbalancing*. **Raising the head hinders** *streamlining* **and** *counterbalancing*. *But you are asking the learner to do exactly what the mind is telling the body not to do.*

HEAD OUT – ARMS IN

There is a **rule of thumb** that I always emphasize with my learners: **"Head Out – Arms In."** **This simply means that if your head is out of the water, your arms should be in the water and positioned in front of the shoulders.** Let us look at the implications for the drowning victim.

Drowning victims have a tendency to extend their arms out to the sides. From this position, they push down on the water in order to push their heads up out of the water to breathe. Very often, they reach and grab at the air as well as slap at the water. Why grab at the air, when only the resistance of water can hold you up?

Conversely, the arms extended in front of the shoulders in the water helps **counterbalance** the legs. If the legs are not **counterbalanced**, the body sinks too far under the water, limiting a swimmer's ability to rhythmically breathe. *The only way to counterbalance the legs when your head is out of the water is by keeping your arms in the water extended in front of the shoulders.* This allows the swimmer to take advantage of the resistance of water, using arm strokes.

THE INSTINCTIVE DROWNING RESPONSE

Frank Pia was a former chief lifeguard at Orchard Beach and is an international authority on water safety. Frank has conducted extensive research studies on the subject of drowning. He has produced an informative water safety video called *THE REASONS PEOPLE DROWN* which includes live actual footage of drowning victims as lifeguards were en route to rescue them. The following is quoted from the Safety Meeting Leader's guide that is used as a supplement to the video:

"Drowning is suffocation in water. . . .In an attempt to avoid suffocation, an *instinctive response* is triggered. **The drowning sequence is as follows.** The victims are in water over their heads, they take in a gulp of air and sink below the surface of the water. They want more air so they push down on the water with their arms extended to their sides. They resurface with their heads tilted back and sink again as their arms extend over their heads. They repeat the sinking - resurfacing sequence pushing down on the water with their arms extended and heads tilted back, until they are rescued or drown."

(For more information contact: L.S.A. Productions, Inc., 3 Boulder Brae Lane, Larchmont, NY 10538. Tel: 914-834-7546. E-Mail: Piaenterpris@macconnect.com)

Now let us return to the **drowning scenario.**

A DROWNING SCENARIO

"I am standing by the edge of the pool. All of a sudden I am falling – falling into the water. I reach out to break the fall. I hit the water. My body is on top of the water. What is happening? Some water went up my nose. My eyes are not seeing like they normally do. I dare not rub them. I am so confused and disoriented. I feel out of control. I lift my head as high and back as possible trying to catch a breath. I reach and grab at the water to my sides and try to push my head above water to breathe. But the water cannot always lift me. I am sinking. I cannot touch the bottom. I need some air but I cannot catch a breath. The horror, I am going to drown."

ANALYSIS

When a victim first falls into the water, his/her natural buoyancy will bring the victim back up to the surface. There is air in the lungs. Air in the lungs gives the body an initial tendency to float. How the victim responds to the initial contact with the water is quite essential.

The drowning victim has just made three critical mistakes:

1. The victim is not kicking because the he/she is trying to touch the bottom with his/her feet. The body is vertical in the water causing the legs to pull the rest of the body under the water.

2. The victim has instinctively extended the arms to the side. Extending the arms to the side inhibits streamlining and counterbalancing which prevents the victim from executing any kind of effective kick.

3. The victim is tilting the head back in order to breathe which further inhibits streamlining and counterbalancing.

Briefly stated, in this case, haste does not make waste. If the swimmer reacts immediately to the drowning scenario, the victim immensely increases the chances of success. What to do? Extend the arms in front of the shoulders and tilt the head down. Streamline the body and counterbalance the sinking legs. Initiate a kick and arm movement of choice.

But what if the victim does not respond correctly? What if the victim allows the legs to sink under the body? What are the implications of not reacting immediately?

THE SWIMMER

As a lifeguard at Orchard Beach I witnessed the following scenario numerous times. A swimmer will be swimming along thinking that the water is not deep. For no apparent reason, the swimmer abruptly stops and tries to stand up. But the swimmer is over his/her head in water that is deeper than expected. The swimmer uses the feet to feel and reach for the bottom. But, reaching for the bottom with the feet makes matters worse since it causes the swimmer to become vertical in the water. **The legs now begin to pull the swimmer under the water.** The swimmer instinctively extends his/her arms out to the side of the shoulders.

Up until this point in time, mind you, the swimmer is under control. But, as soon as the swimmer realizes that the water is deeper than expected, he/she begins to panic. **The swimmer does not know how to start swimming with the body suspended vertically in the water.** Up until this point, swimming always started by touching something solid – such as pushing off a sandy beach bottom or the side of a swimming pool.

Tell-tale signs abound. **Fear is written all over the swimmer's face.** The eyes are opened wide. The movements become quick and disjointed. You can see the total breakdown of the mind-body connection. **The swimmer is in need of immediate assistance.**

The **DROWNING SCENARIO** and the situation whereby the **SWIMMER** realizes the water is deeper than expected are both sudden and unexpected occurrences. Minimal swimming skills are required to water-safe the victims in both instances. *There is a significant difference between starting to swim with your legs on top of the water versus starting to swim with your legs under the water.*

The **SWIMMER** could swim but was not water-safe because he/she could not start swimming with the legs suspended under the water. As we proceed, the reader should understand that it is much easier to swim when you are on top of the water. Starting to swim when your body is vertical in the water requires much more confidence and skill.

Now, it is hoped that the reader has a sense of what the problems are. Let us change our focus to solving the problems themselves.

5
THE READINESS SKILLS

RELAX?

Many instructors encourage learners to begin swimming on their back. The most obvious reason, I guess, is that the learner's face remains out of the water at all times which, in turn, allows the learner to breathe freely at all times. Quite naturally, it is easier to breathe with your face looking away from the water. Learning how to float and a simple backstroke using a sculling arm motion are often the first skills taught.

Let me not mislead the reader. Floating and swimming on your back are invaluable water-safe skills for the learner. There is absolutely nothing wrong with teaching a learner how to swim this way. Many swimming instructors are quite successful using the back method of learning how to swim.

I prefer to have my learners first learn how to swim on their front rather than their back initially. It is the way I learned how to swim as a child and is the method I can best relate to. As far as I am concerned, there is really no right way or wrong way to teach swimming – just preferences. **The sensitivity and teaching skills of the instructor far outweigh any methodology.**

However, the main reason for my reluctance to use the back method of teaching swimming initially is that floating and subsequently swimming on the back requires much more confidence and trust than swimming on the front. The learner must learn how to "*relax*" in the water in order to become proficient at both floating and swimming on the back. But, learning to *relax* in the water is easier said than done. Swimming on the back and floating requires a great deal of one-on-one interaction between the learner and instructor. The ability to *relax* is a water readiness skill from which one can infer that the learner has already made significant strides in facilitating the mind-body connection.

Teaching preferences aside, there are definite advantages to swimming on your stomach, such as the ability to see what is in front of you, under you, and what is to the sides of you. I guess it is really all about a sense of *control* and *orientation*.

Remember, my focus is on the sudden and unexpected events whereby a person finds himself/herself in deep water, and must swim a short distance to safety. Swimming on the front demands that the learner be **pro-active**. The learner has to get moving right away. The face is facing the water. I sense that the fearful swimmer can better respond to a sudden unexpected event on the front rather than on the back since the learner can visually remain in charge. The learner can assess the situation at all times. Not only is he/she better able to see, the learner is better able to hear.

Relaxing is not an option for the at risk swimmer. If the at-risk swimmer is better oriented to the situation visually, he/she is better able to take control of the situation and to take action. **Keep in mind that how the mind responds to fear can either verify or negate any and all prior training.**

REACT!

It has been my experience that it is easier to teach the learner to instinctively *react* to the sudden unexpected event rather than teaching the learner how to *relax*. Instinctively get the body into gear right away. ***Don't think***! **Do**! Focus on what is necessary to complete the mission – not on whether or not you can complete the mission itself.

A pro-active react approach rather than a passive relaxed approach to teaching swimming reaches a broader spectrum of learners. This is not to say that once a learner learns how to relax, the learner's ability to react suffers. Getting some learners to relax, however, can be next to impossible until they experience success.

Success builds confidence and trust. Only confidence and trust enable the learner to relax. Swimming on the front gives the learner more opportunities to experience **success incrementally** inasmuch as each part of the stroke can be broken down and introduced separately in that position. One can always assume that a typical group of learners will be quite mixed ability-wise. A program that stresses **incremental growth** keeps each learner on task.

The ability to react should not be predicated upon the ability to relax. We can describe it as a kind of **fearful-relaxed** continuum. We prefer the learner to relax. ***We command the learner to react!***

INFANTS AND SMALL CHILDREN

The exception is teaching infants and small children. At this point in time in their development, learning to swim on the back makes more sense. Teaching infants, however, is not my area of expertise. I would recommend reading **Teaching Infants How to Swim, by Claire Timmerman** for those people who are interested in teaching babies and very small children how to swim. It is truly a fascinating subject. But for older learners, I prefer to treat swimming on the back and floating as slightly more advanced water competency skills.

WARM-UP

Each time a beginner enters the water, the learner should be allowed to adjust to the swimming environment at his/her own pace. Naturally, safety guidelines and parameters should be well understood and enforced. But it is crucial for the learner to initially experience the water free of outside interference. Let the learner get whatever swimming readiness adjustments he/she needs out of his/her system. The need may be to socialize, to play, to practice a skill, adapt to the water temperature, or just stand there and look around. There is always a need and it should be acknowledged.

The warm-up is also an excellent time for the teacher/ swimmer to assess the needs, improvement or any changes in the learners themselves. *"Sometimes you can observe a whole lot by watching."* Now is the time to fine tune the strategies that you will use that day. This is the critical time in the teacher/swimmer planning phase.

For example, each class that I taught at PS 32 averaged 12-20 swimmers. During the warm-up, I would look for a non-swimmer who I thought was capable of swimming for the first time. I would watch for all the tell-tale signals that gave me the "gut" instinct that this child was *ready* to swim with success. After I finished my demonstration, I would ask, "Who in the class would like to try to demonstrate what I just did for the class?" (I always had a pretty good idea who I wanted "who" to be). My aim was to foster the feeling that what I just did was *"do-able"*. Yet, I am an adult. I am a teacher. I am expected to be able to swim. But, when a **peer** does it – especially for the first time – my demonstration gains instant *credibility*.

HOLDING THE BREATH

Holding your breath is an important water-safe skill. The lungs are like a balloon in the chest. Filling the lungs with air gives the swimmer *buoyancy*. Putting air in the lungs enables the body to become **positively buoyant**. That is, it helps you to float. Letting the air out of the lungs creates **negative buoyancy**. That is, it gives you a tendency to sink. On land there are very few instances whereby a person would hold his/her breath. In the water, however, the possibilities are endless. For some of us, holding our breath is not only a water-safe skill, it is a life-skill.

It is imperative for the learner to become comfortable with holding the breath. A swimmer can swim to safety in many cases just by executing an effective swimming stroke on one breath of air. Accomplished competitive swimmers who swim in the 50 meter freestyle don't even consider taking a breath in what they consider such a short race. **A swimmer can travel a considerable distance on one breath of air.** This is certainly enough air to get you back to the side of a pool, or for that matter – back to a boat – back to a fishing pier – or back to a dock. **Holding your breath is an important water-safe skill.**

THE BOAT RIDE

The year was 1980. A dear friend of both my wife and myself, Louise, came to our house for dinner. After we had finished eating, Louise mentioned that she had not taken a ride on the 25-foot cabin cruiser we had owned for the past two years. It was early October. The night was breezy and cool. The boat was kept on a mooring about 100 yards from the back of our home. We decided to go for a ride. My wife could not join us because our children were young and had to be supervised.

Louise and I rowed to the boat. We climbed aboard, started the engines and chatted while the engines were warming up. After a few minutes, it was time to take a ride. We were engrossed in conversation. I let the lines that connected the boat to the mooring drop into the water. We kept on talking; I put the engine in gear. Suddenly and without warning, I heard a strange noise coming from the back of the boat. The boat had just run over the lines that I had just dropped into the water. The lines were entangled around the propeller and propeller shaft under the boat.

"*Blunder! I can't believe I did this! The price of not paying attention! Now what do I do? I can't leave the boat like this. The wind and current will cause the lines to pull on the propeller as well as the propeller shaft. The propeller shaft attaches to the engine. If the shaft is pulled out, the boat will sink. If I cut the lines, what am I going to use in its place? It is October. It is totally dark. Business hours are over. My only first option is to see if I can undo the mess I created.*"

I jumped into the water off the back of the boat. The water was cold. For the next 20 minutes, I dove under the boat trying to unravel the mess I had created. I could not see a thing. I did everything by feel. Louise assisted from the boat by letting go and keeping tension on the lines as needed. Each time I dove, I would take a deep breath and kept working until I ran out of breath. I would come back up to the surface and rest just long enough to get my next breath. I must have done this 30-40 times. Finally, the lines were free of the propeller and shaft.

I climbed onto the boat. I began to shiver uncontrollably. I dressed as quickly as possible and used towels and everything else I could find to put on. As soon as I was dressed, I suddenly became very warm. I began to sweat profusely. Although the water was cold, I expended so much energy by holding my breath and repeatedly trying to free the lines, I actually raised my body temperature. The speed of the turn around from shivering cold to sweating hot was, to say the least, bizarre.

Why spoil an otherwise nice evening? We decided to take a boat ride anyway and laughed at how disastrous this evening could have been. *But, what would I have done if I could not repeatedly hold my breath despite all of the obstacles?* The ability to hold my breath saved the day. I cannot emphasize enough that holding the breath is an invaluable water-safe skill.

WATER IN THE NOSE

I have a favorite **rule of thumb** that I tell my students: *"Air can only go down your nose - not up your nose"!* The logic for my rule of thumb goes like this. Air occupies the inside of the nostrils. Due to the force of gravity, water pressure is down – not up. **Water, therefore, can only get into your nose when you are on your back – not on your front.** The reader can experience what I am saying by placing a small glass top down in a pot of water. Air remains in the glass; water does not come into the glass. There is no place for the air to go. If it works for the glass, why not for the nose?

I have never had one of my students challenge my rule of thumb. While swimming on the front only some kind of *force* can cause water to go up the nose. Inhaling and an errant splash are cases in point. I am sure that there are exceptions, but this rule of thumb has served me well. If you are not convinced, I would recommend exhaling slowly through the nose when placing your head under water.

GOGGLES AND MASKS

Yes! Yes! Yes! Do wear them! They truly enhance water experiences. When a learner opens the eyes behind the protection of a mask or goggles, he/she sees the underwater environment with clarity. The learner is spared the sensation of water with its many chemicals pressing up against the unprotected eye. Why not wear them? They can only enhance the experience and increase the probability of success.

Let us look at the process in terms of *simultaneously* occurring new experiences. The learner must consciously keep the mouth closed and must hold the breath. The learner must open the eyes when the tendency is to close them. The learner has to maintain his/her balance with the head under water. The learner must trust that somehow water is not going to go shooting up the nose. How many *simultaneously* occurring new experiences do you need? Why deal with visual clarity and eye sensitivity at this time? Masks and goggles make sense.

SOME COMMENTS:

- **Make all strap and nose adjustments before using goggles and masks in the water.**
- **I prefer goggles over masks.** I want my students to get accustomed to water touching the exposed nostrils right away. I prefer a mask, however, to not wearing anything over the eyes.
- **"Cheap is Cheap"** You can purchase brand name goggles such as *Speedo* for under $10. If you buy inexpensive goggles they never seem to fit right. They are difficult to adjust. The materials are of inferior quality and can become a bother to use. The same holds true for masks.
- Goggles can be purchased with a **tint and UV protection**. If you swim out of doors in a sunny environment, use the tinted kind. When indoors or late in the day you are better off with a clear lens. I keep a pair of each.
- Sunscreens can work themselves into the area of the eyes and cause an irritation of the eyes while wearing goggles. **Be careful when applying sunscreen.** Sunscreen can go from hands to goggles or from skin to goggles.
- **Not having goggles or masks is not an impediment to learning.** If a learner is willing to put head under water without goggles or masks, let the learner do it. "No Guts, No Glory". Keep the process moving.

"CATCHER" POSE

The warm-up is over. Now it is time to experience the water together with the learner. My strategy is to teach what I call the "catcher" pose. I tell my learner to allow himself/herself to squat in water above the waist but below the chest and assume a baseball catcher's position – with arms extended and palms down in front of the shoulders. I say, "Just sit on the water. Let your arms lay on top of the water just like you do when you lay your arms on top of a table. Relax. Don't try to hold your arms up."

In order to foster a sense of security, I position the beginner with back facing the sides of the pool. If the learner chooses, the back can even touch the side of the pool itself. The extended arms and buttocks *counterbalance* each other. The buttocks naturally have a tendency to sink. The tendency to sink, however, is **counterbalanced** by the extension of the arms. This pose is very comfortable and easy to maintain.

The benefit of the catcher pose is that the learner can *relax* and safely experience an interaction of the body with the resistance of water. The learner experiences *buoyancy* as well as an additional readiness skill. **The learner is learning to *relax* in the water.**

Facing the student, I engage him/her in a discussion

about the pose itself, or any skills and concepts deemed appropriate at that time. Remember, our mission is to water-safe this learner. We are subtly chipping away at the barriers that hinder the mind-body connection. A simple buoyancy exercise can be viewed as one of the **incremental "successes"** that will *cumulatively* make this connection possible.

HEAD IN THE WATER

From the catcher pose, I tell the learner to crouch further down and place the head in the water just above the eyes to below the top of the forehead. The learner looks straight ahead. From the catcher pose, the learner can move freely up and down resting the back on the wall if necessary. By pushing slowly down on the buttocks, the head lowers under the water. By slowly pushing up on the buttocks, the head lifts out of the water. The learner is supported by the wall behind and is stabilized by the extended arms in the front. The learner is in total control at all times.

OPEN THE EYES

The teacher/swimmer is positioned in front of the learner, also in a catcher pose. This must be a shared experience with the learner. You want the learner to open the eyes underwater and visually face his/her surroundings. The teacher/swimmer should smile and wave to the learner as soon as the learner lowers the head. Rest assured, the learner will be excited and pleasantly surprised. Never allow the learner to close his/her eyes underwater. All you would be doing is reinforcing the fear(s) that causes the learner to want to close the eyes in the first place. In this case, "better untaught than ill taught".

FACE IN THE WATER

Once the learner is comfortable with putting head in the water, it is time for the learner to put face in the water. Starting from a catcher pose, the learner lifts the buttocks, leans slightly forward and looks face down at the water. From this position the learner lifts the chin (not the head), further bends the knees and places the head/face in the water. The learner should re-position the feet or place one foot against the wall to maintain balance. Pretend that there is a "middle-aged" bald spot on the top of the head that you want to keep dry. The learner is looking down and forward. We do the same in water as we do on land. You want to see what is under you and what is in front of you.

THE PRONE GLIDE

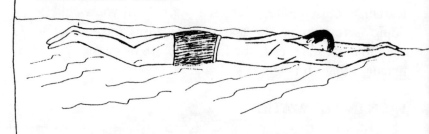

It is now time for the learner to experience what it is like to be *suspended* **in water horizontally.** It is time to experience *streamlining*. It is time to **Let Go**! It is time to learn the prone glide.

STREAMLINING

By way of introduction, I ask my students to focus on a kickboard. If you place a kickboard horizontally on top of the water and gently push it, the kickboard is quite easily propelled in the direction it is pushed. If you take this same kickboard and place it vertically in the water, it requires two hands using considerable force to push it. By way of analogy, the body works the same way. The more of the body is on top of the water, the less effort required to propel it. The more of the body is under the water, the more effort required to propel it – if it can be done at all. **Streamlining the body counteracts the resistance of water.**

COUNTERBALANCE

The legs give a body a tendency to sink. The lungs when filled with air give a body a tendency to float. But let us consider the arms for a moment. As mentioned earlier, if you extend the arms forward, you help **counterbalance** the legs. The arms, which are made of muscle and bone, have a tendency to sink just like the legs. Just as the arms counterbalance the buttocks in the catcher pose, they counterbalance the legs when extended. Extending the arms not only helps counterbalance the legs, but when done in conjunction with extending the legs, streamlines the body.

EXECUTION

So far, the student has learned the catcher pose, putting head and face in the water. Building upon these skills, the steps for the prone glide are as follows:

1. Assume the catcher pose.
2. Lift the buttocks and lean forward.
3. Lift the chin and have the face looking down and forward.
4. Place one foot on the wall.
5. Take a deep slow breath. Exhale.
6. Take a deep slow breath. Exhale.
7. Take a deep breath.
8. Bend the knees and lower the face into the water.
    (Keep the middle-aged bald spot dry).
9. Push off the wall.
10. Keep arms extended in front of the shoulders, angled in, never out.
11. Straighten the legs.
12. Keep legs together.
13. Point the toes.
14. As you slow down, lift the head, and bend the knees. Gently push down with the extended arms.
15. Assume a catcher pose.

TWO DEEP BREATHS

There is a physical as well as a psychological reason for taking two deep breaths before taking a final breath. By taking two deep breaths, you expand the lungs allowing the lungs to take in more air on the subsequent breath. As a result, you can take in more air and hold your breath longer. Taking two deep breaths is also an anxiety reliever. It is no different than when a speaker takes a deep breath at the podium before starting a speech. It helps relieve the tension.

DEMONSTRATION

If we lived in an ideal world, the prone glide sequentially would be the next step up the ladder of water competence. But, we do not live in an ideal world. Many learners at this point will not let go and execute a prone glide. It is much too passive an activity. The mind of the learner insists that it be more pro-active. The learner prefers to move and not relax. This does not preclude the learner from learning the prone glide at some future time.

The learner's unwillingness to try a prone glide should not be viewed as a hindrance to progress. The instructor demonstrating the prone glide, on the other hand, is critical to the learner's understanding of streamlining and counterbalancing. The demonstration of the prone glide can stand on its own as a teaching strategy. Demonstrating the prone glide enables the learner to gain visual insights into how the body can move in water. Keep on chipping away until the mind and body connect.

TEACHING TIP
Go slowly, whenever you demonstrate a swimming skill. Emphasis must always be on *form,* not *speed!*
The mind must be given time to process what it sees.

6
OVERHAND ARM STROKE

The overhand arm stroke is the stroke used in the **crawl** or what is sometimes called the *freestyle* swimming stroke. The **crawl** is the fastest swimming stroke, as well as the most powerful and efficient stroke. The **crawl** is not terribly hard to learn and is probably the most practical swimming stroke to know. Most people, I believe, identify swimming with the **crawl,** whether it be from watching a swimming race, an ironman competition, or someone attempting to swim the English Channel.

The key to learning the **crawl** is to develop a proficient arm stroke. The legs provide streamlining and stability to the body. The arms provide the real propulsion. The movement we use to maximize this propulsion is the overhand arm stroke.

STEPS AND COMMENT
The following steps are my method of teaching the overhand arm stroke:

1. Slice. Place your hand into the water in front of your shoulders – elbow up – the thumb pointing slightly down.

2. **Reach.** Extend your arm forward until it is fully extended in front of the shoulder under water.

OVERHAND ARM STROKE
(FOCUS ON *LEFT* ARM)

SLICE AND REACH

GRAB

PULL

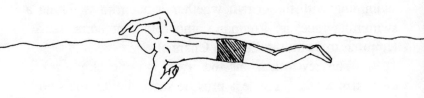

TOUCH

LIFT AND ROLL

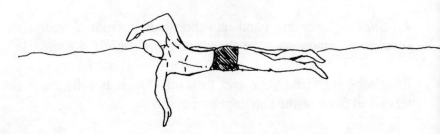

3. *Grab*. Grab the water using that portion of your arm from the hand to the elbow.

COMMENT: Some instructors recommend bending your wrist down at this point. I prefer my swimmers to keep their wrists firm but flexible and doing what comes naturally.

4. *Pull*. Pull the water from the front of your body to the back of your body at an increasing speed.

SCULLING: Some instructors recommend that the swimmer move the arm in an "out-in-out" or "sculling" motion. It is often referred to as the S stroke. I prefer to allow my learners to do what comes naturally. It has been my experience that as the learner builds up confidence, the various parts of the body begin to relax and an "out-in-out" pattern begins to develop naturally in response to the resistance of the water. The learner instinctively begins to realize that the more water he/she can grab and hold onto the more effective the overhand arm stroke becomes. There is plenty of room for trial and error at this point. Be assured, the body responds rhythmically in kind as the mind-body connection develops.

RIGHT ANGLE: Some instructors recommend that swimmers have the hand at a right angle to the elbow when the pull reaches and passes the shoulders. I do not stress this point, preferring my students to take advantage of the *natural flex of the elbow* as the student pulls the water from the front of the body to the back of the body. The important points to remember are that the elbow is relaxed and always higher than the hand.

5. *Touch*. The stroke continues until the thumb touches the outside of the thigh.

COMMENT: The arm should travel no further than the thigh or else it gets what I call "*stuck*" and the swimmer has to drop the elbow in order to lift arm out of the water.

6. *Lift and roll.* Immediately lift the hand out of the water as the thumb touches the thigh and roll the shoulder forward.

COMMENT: Make the lift and roll one continuous motion.

OVERVIEW

To the best of my knowledge, there are really no other movements of the arms and shoulders that can be compared to the overhand arm stroke. Essentially, the overhand arm stroke is a continuous alternating movement of the arms in and out of the water facilitated by the rolling of the shoulders. Keep in mind that it is imperative that the swimmer never drop the elbow. **Proper execution of the overhand arm stroke requires the elbow to always be higher than the hand throughout the stroke.**

ASSOCIATION

The biggest stumbling block for the learner is that there is really no point of reference for the overhand arm stroke. As the reader will soon surmise, the overhand arm stroke is a series of movements that the body is just not accustomed to doing. There are really no "just likes" to use for comparison. The mind and body connect best through association. What movements can you associate with the overhand arm stroke?

Let me explain further. If you wanted to teach a child who knows how to throw a ball, how to hit a ball, you can say, "Place the weight of your body on your back foot, 'just like' when you throw a ball."

"Swing the bat across your body, shifting your weight from your back foot to your front foot, 'just like' when you throw a ball."

"Follow through with the bat, 'just like' when you throw a ball."

"A 'righty' batter should step forward with the left foot – a 'lefty' should step with the right foot, 'just like' when you throw a ball."

"Don't be afraid to snap your wrists, 'just like' when you throw a ball."

Through association a learner can be readily taught how to hit a ball, borrowing from the knowledge and experience the learner gained from learning how to throw a ball.

There is no comparable model, however, of movement associations for the overhand arm stroke. As a result, mastering the movements of the overhand arm stroke should be learned before attempting to use the arm stroke in a **"try to swim"** situation. It simply does not come naturally for most people. It is no different than when a pilot learns how to fly in a simulator. **Familiarity with the movement enhances and, in most cases, guarantees the probability of success.**

Most beginners tend to "rock" their shoulders when attempting the overhand arm stroke initially, a kind of swinging of their arms and shoulders. This is a clear indication that they are tightening their arms and shoulder joints. Tightening at the shoulder joints should only take place during the **pull** phase of the overhand arm stroke. The **pull** phase is when the arms are using the resistance of water to propel the body. The swimmer instinctively tightens the shoulders to pull the water back. The arms continue to remain relaxed.

VISUALIZATION

A learner can visualize swimming in the water. I always encourage my learners to practice the arm movements at home in front of a mirror, imagining that they are actually swimming in the water. By visualizing the arm movements, the learner can master the rhythm of the arm stroke before trying to execute the arm stroke in the water.

Visualization helps the learner gain in confidence. **When it comes time for the learner to execute an arm stroke in a "try to swim" situation, the learner is better able to trust the body to respond effectively to the task at hand.**

The ability to model a movement varies from individual to individual. The eyes see. The mind processes. The body imitates. The result, as you might expect, is a wide range of outcomes. Not all learners have the ability to model what is shown to them right away. They should be given time to develop the *"feel"* for what it is to move their arms effectively in the water.

Just think about it for a moment. There is much involved in the proper execution of the overhand arm stroke. The shoulder rolls freely. The arms alternate moving opposite to and independent of each other. The hand slices the water in front of the shoulder thumb down and the arm is extended under the water. **The elbow is always higher than the hand and remains bent during the stroke.** As the learner touches the thigh with the thumb of one hand, the opposite hand is entering the water. The head should be looking down and forward.

By mastering this unfamiliar movement beforehand, the learner is better able to execute the stroke effectively. The probability of success increases immensely. *Experiencing success is the key to mastering the mind-body connection.*

The technique I use to help the learner better visualize the overhand arm stroke is as follows: I ask the learner to pretend that he/she is swimming in a pool wearing goggles with the eyes open. I ask the learner to place the **hands on the knees,** keeping the face down, being especially careful not to put the chin on the chest. I ask the learner to **lift the chin - not the head**. By keeping the hands on the knees, it is most difficult to lift the head.

In effect, I am telling the learner that you are **looking down and slightly forward**. Your intention is to see what is under you and what is in front of you. *I stress to the learner that it is imperative that you lift the chin only – not the head.*

At this point, I ask the learner to imagine grabbing the water from the front of the body and pulling it toward the back of the body. As one arm goes in the water, the other arm comes out of the water. **The elbow is always higher than the hand.** Concentrate on trying to relax and roll the shoulders forward with a steady hand entry. Both arms do the same movement but move opposite and independent of each other. The continuous rhythmic movement of pulling the water from the front of the body to the back of the body propels the body forward.

I ask the learner to look down and keep the head slightly above the water and to concentrate on how pulling the water back pushes the body forward. I encourage the learner to develop a *"feel"* for what it is when the arms and hands make contact with the water. *Concentrate on the feel of the water rushing past your leg.* In some cases, I ask the learner to begin walking with the arms and hands doing most of the work. Using an overhand arm stroke, can best be described as pulling your body through water using your arms and hands – especially your hands – for power.

COMMANDS

By way of introduction, I ask the learner to allow the arms to dangle from the shoulders and to shake the hands similar to what a swimmer does before beginning a race. My commands are as follows:

- "Keep your arms and shoulders relaxed."
- "Don't rock your shoulders, roll your shoulders."
- "Don't swing your arms, reach out in front of your shoulders with a steady arm entry."

- "Arms move opposite and independent of each other."
- "Don't lift your head, keep your head looking down and slightly forward."
- **"Don't drop your elbows, always keep them higher than your hands."**
- "Touch the outside of your leg with your thumb and immediately lift your arm up."

HOMEWORK

For homework, I ask my learners to practice the overhand arm stroke at home in front of a mirror. I never consider such a request frivolous. *Becoming comfortable with the movement enables the learner to trust the body when it becomes time to learn how to swim with the head in the water.* The learner has enough "baggage" such as fear and inexperience with which to deal. Mastering the movements helps build the confidence the learner needs to take risks. *Mastering movements increases probability of success.*

LOCK - UNLOCK

It is important for the learner to understand that the head should be looking down in order to maximize the reach of the arm. I use the terms **"Lock"** and **"Unlock"** to stress the importance of keeping your head looking down. Raising the head **"locks"** the shoulders, restricting the arm reach. Lowering the head **"unlocks"** the shoulders, extending the arm reach. The reader can experience the lock and unlock feeling by simulating the overhand arm stroke while looking down at the floor and gradually lifting the head. As you lift the head, the reach of the arm becomes restricted. *It is important for the learner to understand how various parts of the body interact when we move.* This in turn gives a sense of the feel of the movement. Using the terms **"Lock"** and **"Unlock"** keeps it simple.

UNIVERSAL STROKE

Lifting the head inhibits the reach of the arm forward. Lowering the head allows the shoulder to reach forward - which in turn allows the arm to reach forward. There are some swimmers who swim what I consider the **"universal"** stroke; that is, they turn their head from side to side each time they take an arm stroke. It can be a very effective method of swimming since *turning* your head from side to side with each arm stroke is in and of itself not a problem.

Swinging your head from side to side is another story. Most people who swing their head from side to side keep their head too high, the elbows too low and are not rolling the shoulders forward. Their head, arms and shoulders tend to swing together in a kind of "bouncing, bobbing" motion. The end result is **frustration**.

Interestingly, the universal stroke is the most common stroke among untaught swimmers. As a point of information, the reasons, I believe are as follows:

* The swimmer is able to keep the head out of the water at all times.
* It allows the shoulders to **unlock,** which in turn allows the arms and hands to move more freely.
* It is probably the most modeled stroke among young people.

ASSISTANCE

If a learner is having difficulty developing a feel for the movement of the overhand arm stroke, there are some techniques that can be used to overcome this problem.

• *Step 1.* Stand in front of the learner in the water. Hold the learner's wrists and try to simulate the movement of the overhand arm stroke. Basically at this point, you are trying to give the learner a sense of how the shoulders roll continuously, freely and independent of each other.

• *Step 2.*   Stand alongside the learner and hold the learner's elbow and hand. Insist that the learner relax the arm. You are swimming – not boxing. Simulate the overhand arm stroke movement with one arm only. Repeat as follows: *"REACH – GRAB – PULL"*. Substitute the expression: *"HAND - WRIST - ELBOW"* **to emphasize the importance of keeping the elbow higher than the hand.** Encourage the learner to feel the water rushing past the leg. Make the learner's thumb touch the outside of the thigh and immediately lift the arm out of the water. Now ask the learner to try and coordinate the arm stroke with you using the opposite arm.

THE ELBOW MUST ALWAYS BE HIGHER THAN THE HAND

There is a natural inclination to keep the elbow lower than the hand. Throwing and typing are cases in point. **A swimmer must always keep the elbow higher than the hand or else the overhand arm stroke will be totally ineffective.** A suggested method of dealing with this problem is to ask the learner to pretend that the arms are reaching over a barrow each time he/she executes an overhand arm stroke. If the elbow is too low, the forearm will bang into the barrow. Hopefully, the learner will focus on the association and make a conscious effort to keep the elbow higher than the hand.

PRACTICE

There is not much more that you can do at this point. It is up to the learner to practice the movement. Never forget that learning to swim is a process – not a product. **The desire to take a chance to learn how to swim must be internal, not external.** There is nothing wrong with measuring success incrementally. Learning the movement must be viewed as a lead-up skill. **The learner is learning how** to swim. The issue is, if and when the learner is ready and willing to take the plunge.

TAKING THE PLUNGE

"This is it! The moment I have been waiting for. I am for the first time allowing myself to LET GO. That's right. LET GO. I am not going to be touching something solid for the first time in my entire life. I am not going to drown. I am not going to choke. Water is not going up my nose. I am going to open my eyes. I am going to hold my breath. I am going to push off the wall with my foot. I am going to straighten my legs. I am going to keep my legs together. I am going to point my toes back. I am going to take 10 strokes and pull myself to the other side of the pool. I am scared to death. "

SAFETY ALERT

It is very important that a beginning swimmer's first attempt to swim be in water that is not over his/her head. This may seem obvious, but let us not take anything for granted. I would say that waist high water to just below the chest is the ideal depth from which the learner takes the plunge.

CONSIDERATIONS:

1. The learner should be comfortable with putting the head/face under the water.
2. A learner should know that it is important to keep eyes open underwater at all times. *(A well fitted pair of swimming goggles or mask is a real plus.)*
3. The learner must understand that the head must stay in the water looking down and forward.

The learner must resist the temptation to put the chin on the chest. *If you see that the learner is pressing chin to chest, you can pretty much assume that the learner is also closing the eyes.* The learner may not be ready to take the plunge, but should be practicing putting the head in the water to build up confidence.

4. The learner must be comfortable with holding the breath. Remember that two deep breaths prior to holding your breath is a stress reliever as well as increases the amount of air you can take into your lungs.

5. Does the learner know how to do the prone glide?

6. Can the learner do the "Flutter" kick?

Please note: Items 5 and 6 are extremely helpful skills when learning the overhand arm stroke, but are not essential skills. Once again, it depends upon the learner as to whether one or both of these skills should be learned prior to taking the plunge.

HOW TO TAKE THE PLUNGE

1. Assume a catcher's pose.
2. Lift the buttocks and lean forward.
3. Lift chin and have face looking down and forward.
4. Keep both arms out in front of you, shoulder width apart, angled in, never out.
5. Place one foot on the wall.
6. Take a deep slow breath. Exhale.
7. Take a deep slow breath. Exhale.
8. Take a deep slow breath.
9. Bend the knees and lower the face into the water. *(Keep the middle-aged bald spot dry).*
10. Hold your breath.
11. Push off the wall with one foot.
12. Straighten the legs.
13. Keep your legs together.
14. Point your toes back.
15. Pull back on one arm.
16. Begin the overhand arm stroke.
17. Count 10 arm strokes.

TEN STROKES

The PS32 pool is 18' wide. Rather than tell my learners to swim from one side to the other, I tell them to take 10 strokes, assuring them that it is quite easy if they take a deep breath and hold it. Invariably, the person taking the plunge reaches the other side of the pool in less than 10 strokes.

The advantage in presenting the challenge this way is that the learner focuses on the count and not on the goal. By focusing on the count, the learner is, in essence, focusing on the arm stroke. The learner is now concentrating on technique – not on success or failure. The learner is no longer burdened with the fear of whether or not he/she will make it to the other side of the pool. By counting, the insecure thoughts are momentarily distracted. The mind and body briefly connect. The learner experiences success. The "baggage" is starting to be discarded.

LUIGI

I stumbled upon my 10 stroke method by teaching swimming to a boy named Luigi. Luigi was in the 5th grade. At the time, I would try to schedule swimming for each child about 10 times per year. Luigi was always present. He was a terrific **"land" swimmer**. That is, he knew all of the movements, but was unwilling to **"LET GO."** Each time he would attempt to swim, he would abruptly stop and put his feet on the bottom. He felt too out of control and disoriented to let go.

Getting Luigi to **"LET GO"** perplexed me. I would demonstrate over and over. But still, Luigi did not want to **"LET GO".** Finally, I said to him, "Luigi, I just want you to take 10 strokes."

I made no further requests. I assured him that it was okay to stop after 10 strokes. Luigi nodded his head. Seven strokes later he reached the other side of the pool. He leaped out of the pool making a V gesture with his arms as if he had just won the Olympic gold. His face was beaming. I was witnessing a defining moment in this young boy's life. The ultimate teacher **"rush"**.

More importantly, however, I gained a new and lasting insight into how to teach the fearful learner – a kind of "bait and switch" technique that I would use effectively over and over again. Instead of addressing the fear head-on, let us see if we can run around it by distracting the child from the fear. The outcome remains the same. Our goal has been met once the mind-body connection has been facilitated.

TO KICK OR NOT TO KICK

It depends. *If the legs are not in synch with the arm stroke, propulsion is actually impeded when you kick.* Pushing off the wall, straightening the legs, pointing the toes back and keeping the legs together is really all you need to do at this point. Trial and error is probably the real answer to this question.

PRONE GLIDE

If the learner can comfortably execute the prone glide, learning the overhand arm stroke is much easier. The learner has already demonstrated a willingness to **"LET GO."** The transition from a prone glide to an overhand arm stroke is a natural progression. At this point technique becomes the primary consideration, and as discussed earlier, there are some learners who are unwilling to relax enough to learn the prone glide. They need to be more pro-active in the water in order to make the mind-body connection. These learners are better off learning the overhand arm stroke before the prone glide.

SUMMARY

The learner at this point has achieved a **milestone** in water competency – swimming for the first time in his/her entire life.   Does this mean that the learner is water-safe? Absolutely not! The learner has learned to swim in shallow water with the legs starting out on top of the water. There is still a long way to go. But, the learner has begun to put into place a new personal **paradigm shift**. Learning how to swim is not so far-fetched. **Learning how to swim is "doable."**

7
FLUTTER KICK

The term flutter kick is a misnomer. The leg neither flutters nor kicks. The flutter kick is an alternating motion of the legs up and down similar to the way we move our legs when we walk. Just as in walking, the flutter kick begins at the hip with a relaxed knee and ankle. The essential difference is in how we position our foot. When we walk, the body is vertical and the foot is kept at a 90° angle to the leg. When we swim, the body is horizontal and the foot attempts to achieve a 180° angle to the leg, similar to how a ballerina stands on her toes. From this position, the swimmer makes contact with the water using the top of the foot. Only in this way can the swimmer take full advantage of the density of water to resist the foot.

FLEXION

But not everybody has the flexibility in the ankle to achieve a 180° angle with their foot. Therefore, the swimmer must now compensate for this inflexibility by slightly flexing the knees. By slightly bending the knees, the swimmer will now be able to make contact with the water, using the entire surface of the top of the foot. It is essential that both the ankles and feet be totally relaxed to maximize the benefits of the flexion in the ankles. In this way, the rhythm of the kick will develop much more naturally.

POWER

The power of the flutter kick originates from that portion of the leg below the knee. The flutter kick is not a stiff-knee movement. Not only does the knee compensate for the lack of flexion in the ankle, but the knee leads the kick on both the downswing and upswing. The knee flexes on the downswing and straightens on the upswing causing the leg to become straight as it comes back toward the surface of the water. On the other hand, the movement of the leg from the hip to the knee allows more for stability and body alignment rather than for power.

POINTS TO REMEMBER

1. The legs should remain in the water at all times.
2. There should be some churning of the water near the surface with only the heel of the foot actually breaking the surface of the water.
3. The legs should be kept together at all times.
4. The legs should be straight except for a slight flexing of the knees on the downswing.
5. The ankles should be relaxed.
6. Concentrate on pressing down with the top part of your foot.
7. The alternating leg movement should be continuous.
8. The kick should be shallow, and the legs should travel no more than 6"-18" under the surface of the water.

HOW I TEACH THE FLUTTER KICK
STREAMLINE THE SWIMMER

Surrounding the PS32 pool is an overflow gutter which allows for the surface water to overflow into the gutter. The overflow gutter is helpful in removing hair and any other debris floating on the surface of the pool. It is also a very effective teaching aid. I have my learner place the hands over the edge of the overflow and extend the arms. Simultaneously, I grab the learner's feet. I straighten the legs and hold the feet placing my thumb on the sole of the foot with my fingers on the top of the foot (instep). **I caution my learner to relax the neck and not try to lift the head too high – allow the chin to touch the surface of the water.** Since the overflow is at the water surface level, the learner's body is now *streamlined* similar to how the body should be positioned while swimming.

FLUTTER KICK
LEFT LEG - DOWNSWING
RIGHT LEG - UPSWING

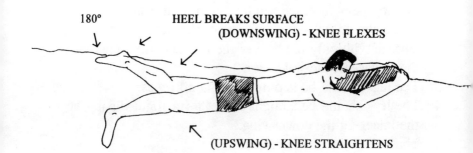

180°   HEEL BREAKS SURFACE
         (DOWNSWING) - KNEE FLEXES

(UPSWING) - KNEE STRAIGHTENS

SIMULATE THE KICK

As I sense that the learner is becoming comfortable in this *streamlined* position, I begin to rotate the learner's feet front and back with my hands. If I feel the learner's ankles stiffening up and resisting me, I tell the learner, **"Too Stiff"** or **"Relax the Ankles."** I keep this up until the learner does relax the ankles. When the ankles relax, the legs relax.

Once the learner relaxes the ankles, I begin to simulate the flutter kick by moving the learner's legs up and down. I tell the learner to **"point your toes back"** and try to **"hit on the top part of the foot."** I assist the learner by trying to produce the proper flexion of the knee, which enables him/her to hit the water with the top part of the foot. Meanwhile

I physically move the learner's legs up and down.

If the learner relaxes and does not resist me, I can quite effectively have this young swimmer experience the "**feel**" of the flutter kick. **Focus on the ankle.** Generally speaking (and to repeat), when the learner relaxes the ankle, the entire leg will also relax. The feel of the flutter kick can be best described as a "floppy" leg movement.

The next step is to stand alongside the learner and place my front hand under the learner's knee and the back hand under the learner's foot. I simulate the kick with one leg while at the same time asking the learner to simulate the kick with the opposite leg. **Do not allow the learner to stiffen the leg.** Once again, the goal is to have the learner experience the "**feel**" of the flutter kick.

KICKBOARD

Practicing with a kickboard is very helpful in learning the flutter kick. It must be stressed, however, that **a kickboard is a teaching aid – not a floatation device**. The learner should not be allowed to bend the elbows and try to climb on the kickboard which many beginners have a tendency to do. **The learner's arms should be kept straight with the elbows maintaining contact with the kickboard at all times.** The hands should be positioned toward the front and sides of the kickboard. **The head should be kept low in order for the learner to** *streamline* **the body.**

If the learner is not yet comfortable enough to practice with a kickboard, I leave the learner alone, and encourage practice by the side of the pool. A teacher/swimmer should never forget that it took years of positive and negative experiences to bring the learner to this point in life. Fear is a factor with which to contend. Besides, not all learners have the same athleticism or risk-taking threshold. **The focus should always be on the process – not the product.**

PRONE GLIDE

Holding the breath and executing a prone glide is an excellent way to develop a feel for the flutter kick. Starting a kick from a glide allows the learner to ease into a relaxed steady rhythm with the legs. Initially, the beginner should push off the wall just as you would with a prone glide and immediately execute a shallow kick. The beginner's goal, at this point is for the kick to enhance the glide rather than to be a propulsive force. The push-off should be the main propulsive force. Once the swimmer becomes comfortable with the feel of the kick, he/she can now practice a prone glide with a kick without using a push-off.

SWIM FINS

Swim fins are an excellent teaching aid for the more problematic learner. The learner can use swim fins with a kickboard while learning the flutter kick. Swim fins are very helpful teaching aids since they require the learner to actually maintain the proper leg/foot position in the water. Propulsion is only achieved when the learner is actually using correct flutter kick form. Swim fins, however, should be viewed as a last resort for the beginning learner. Swim fins should supplement, not supplant learning the flutter kick.

TAKE NOTHING FOR GRANTED

The physical manipulation of the knee, ankle and foot is quite helpful in trying to help the beginning swimmer make the mind-body connection. There are times, however, when I demonstrate the kick to a group and ask them to try it themselves. Many of my learners instinctively point their toes toward the bottom of the pool. Although their body is horizontal in the water, they kick as they kick on land. They are not visually or mentally making the connection. Naturally, there is no resistance and their legs sink to the bottom.

BENT KNEE KICK

Very often, beginners will use a kick that requires them to bend their knees as much as 90° *out of the water*. Some instructors teach this kick as a lead-up kick to the flutter kick. Personally, I do not recommend this. It has been my experience that it is easier to teach the flutter kick directly rather than teaching a transition from a bent knee kick to a flutter kick.

8
CRAWL

ARMS AND LEGS WORKING TOGETHER

The time has come to have the overhand arm stroke and the flutter kick move together in synch. There are two methods: the two-beat crawl and the six-beat crawl. The two-beat crawl means that you kick your legs two times for each arm stroke cycle, kicking with your opposite leg each time you take an arm stroke. If you stroke with your right arm, you kick with your left leg and vice-versa. The six-beat crawl means that you kick your legs six times for each arm stroke cycle. That is you kick three times on each arm stroke. Most young learners seem to prefer the six beat crawl.

THE SIX-BEAT CRAWL

Basically, the young swimmer prefers to be **pro-active** while learning how to swim. The learner is not relaxed enough to kick just one time each time he/she takes an arm stroke. The learner prefers to kick more rapidly. The problem is coordinating the arm stroke with the kick.

Initially, the learner should concentrate on the arm stroke, focusing on the pull and subsequent glide. The kick, in turn, should enhance this movement. When not in synch with the arm stroke, the kick can actually inhibit the glide. That is why when I answered the earlier question whether to kick or not to kick when learning the overhand arm stroke, I answered, "It depends." *If the kick enhances the glide, then kick. If the kick inhibits the glide, minimize the kick or don't kick at all.* I prefer my learners to use a very easy shallow kick at first. **The emphasis should be to use the legs for streamlining and stability – not for propulsion.**

The best way to practice the six-beat crawl is to count 1-2-3 - 4-5-6 over and over again. In time, arm speed and leg speed begin to develop a natural rhythm. When the arms and legs develop a natural rhythm, the kick enhances the glide. The overhand arm stroke and flutter kick are now in synch. How do we get our arms and legs to move in synch? **Practice! Practice! Practice!**

A SIGN OF SUCCESS

Many young swimmers as they gain confidence will: – stop – lift their heads up – take a breath – put their heads down and continue swimming. The only problem with this technique is that when you lift your head in front of you, your legs will momentarily begin to sink. Therefore, you have to work a little harder to get the body *streamlined* again. On the plus side, this technique can be quite effective for short distances and is used by swimmers who are well underway to making the mind-body connection. To me, it is a pretty good confidence indicator. **Lifting your head in front of you to take a breath, therefore, can be considered an important water-safe skill for short distances.** Swimming for distance, however, requires the development of rhythmic breathing skills.

RHYTHMIC BREATHING

Eventually, all swimmers need air. Ideally, the body should remain *streamlined* each time a swimmer takes a breath. **The swimmer can remain *streamlined* by turning the head to the side rather than lifting it up for a breath.**

Once the learner is comfortable with the overhand arm stroke and flutter kick, it is time to learn breathing from the side rather than from the front.

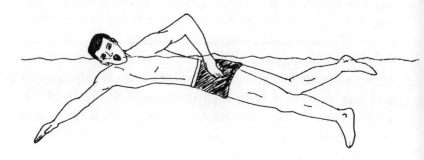

SAME SIDE

A learner should be asked on which side he/she prefers to take a breath. The learner should be told that each breath should be taken only after an even number of arm strokes. That is, 2-4-6, etc. Each two arm strokes is an arm stroke cycle, which means the swimmer will always be turning the head to the same side to take a breath. An odd number of strokes 1-3-5-etc. causes the learner to keep on changing sides to take a breath. It is much easier to learn how to take a breath on one side only. **Switching sides to take a breath should be viewed as a more advanced skill.**

I suggest to new swimmers that they should take a breath on a four (4) count. That is 1-2-3-4, take a breath. The first stroke (1) always starts on the same side as the side you want to take a breath on – the breathing side. The count begins when the arm first enters the water. The cadence should be no faster than 1-one thousand, 2-one thousand, 3-one thousand, 4-one thousand. Give the body a chance to respond to the movement.

ROTATION OF THE UPPER BODY

The hips rotate enough to allow the upper body to rotate sufficiently enough to comfortably take a breath from the side without raising the head. Therefore, on stroke **# 4** I say, **"Drop your shoulder. Lift your elbow. Take a breath."**

ASSISTANCE

Just as with the overhand arm stroke, practicing the movement before actually using it in a **"try to swim"** situation is most helpful. A learner can be assisted by your standing in front of him/her and moving the arms just as with the overhand arm stroke. The difference is that on stroke **# 4** pull down on the elbow of the non-breathing side (this causes the shoulder to drop) and lift the elbow on the breathing side. The learner, at the same time, turns the head on the breathing side, takes a breath, and turns the head back down into the water. **Repeat: "1-2-3-4-take a breath."**

PULL

The pull on the breathing side remains the same. Raising the elbow on the breathing side and dropping the shoulder on the non-breathing side places the arm on the non-breathing side under the *centerline of the body*. The pull on the non-breathing side now takes place under the body on stroke **# 4**. Everything else remains the same.

Please note that when using a body roll, the pull of each arm stroke is always under the *centerline of the body*. During the early stages of learning the overhand arm stroke, I do not stress the importance of the body roll. Most learners simply pull their arms straight back. "It works." It "does not work," when you are trying to take a breath on the side. If you try to rhythmically breathe with the non-breathing side arm pulling straight back, the turn of the head to the breathing side is inhibited. **The body roll and subsequent pull of the non-breathing side arm under the** *centerline of the body* **is essential to taking a breath on the side.** *(A breathing side body roll is optional)*

BREATHING

The learner should hold the breath. As the learner turns the head on stroke **# 4,** he/she should exhale rapidly and take a **deep breath with the mouth only**. This exchange of air should take place every **four** strokes while the head is **out of the water.** Very often beginners will lift their head up before turning their head to take a breath. This is not necessary and should be discouraged.

TIMING

The exchange of air should take place just as the **non-breathing** side begins the *reach,* just before the *grab* and as the **breathing** side *lifts* and *rolls*. The learner may be temporarily out of synch since he/she now must include a breath movement with the overhand arm stroke and flutter kick movements. How does the learner get back into synch? **Practice! Practice! Practice!**

SUMMARY
- The learner should decide on which side to take a breath.
- The learner should take a breath every **4** strokes.
- The learner should exhale rapidly and inhale rapidly through the mouth with the head out of the water.

USE THE COMMANDS:
1. "1-2-3-4-Drop your shoulder – Lift your elbow – Take a breath."
2. "1-2-3-4-take a breath".

COMMENT:
Rhythmic breathing requires considerable practice before it becomes second nature to the swimmer. Many beginning swimmers who suddenly and unexpectedly find themselves suspended in deep water are not quite ready to use rhythmic breathing as a water competency skill. Fear inhibits the mind and body from connecting in these instances. They should simply take a deep breath, place their head down, extend the arms and do an overhand arm stroke and flutter kick to safety.

9
DOGGIE PADDLE

A number of years ago two young women were visiting from Denmark. English was their second language. They were sight-seeing in mid-town Manhattan and kept on seeing the sign "NO STANDING." They interpreted the sign literally and thought that they had to keep on walking. Why not? Everyone they saw was walking at a fast pace.

They walked and they walked from corner to corner. They were desperate to stop and rest, becoming more and more frustrated and fatigued. They were frantic. They kept on seeing the dreaded sign, "NO STANDING." What scary fate awaited them if they stopped walking and decided to stop for a minute and stand? They could not take the chance. They had to keep on walking. Finally, out of desperation they ducked into a store to get a much needed respite. Needless to say, that they were quite embarrassed when they realized that the sign referred to automobiles – not pedestrians.

LYNCH PIN

The ability to stop – to rest – to assess – to plan is the *lynch pin* of water competency. At this point, can we assume that the learner can swim? Yes! Is the learner water competent? No! The learner has made tremendous strides in facilitating the mind-body connection. The learner can streamline. The learner can put the face in the water. The learner opens the eyes. The learner is willing to "LET GO."

The learner has mastered the strokes and kicks to some degree and has experienced success. Possibly, the learner can take a breath on one side. **But what happens if the learner "STOPS?"** Will he/she have the poise to start up again and continue? Or, will everything mentally fall apart, placing the learner at risk of drowning? The answer to both questions is *Maybe*.

If the learner is not sure of what the learner should, could, or would do if he/she suddenly stops swimming, the mind-body connection is at risk of breaking down. Each learner is an individual. How the mind processes and the body responds produces many different outcomes. Some learners instinctively rise to the occasion, others do not.

So far the mind-body connection is no different from the two Danish girls who felt compelled to keep on walking when they saw the "NO STANDING" sign. They knew the words but did not understand the context in which they were being used. Swimming at this point is also out of context. Our focus has been more skill driven and confidence building. Just as the Danish girls were intimidated by the "NO STANDING" sign and kept walking, the learner feels compelled to swim until the he/she drops. Consequently, the focus must now shift toward what to do if the learner is forced to STOP, to give the mastery of swimming skills the proper context.

THE COMPETENT SWIMMER

The competent swimmer realizes that NOTHING is going to happen if the swimmer should suddenly decide to or need to STOP. Stopping is never an issue. The issues for the competent swimmer are tides, currents, waves, winds, distance, depth, endurance, health, strength and skills. The competent swimmer stops. The competent swimmer remains buoyant. The competent swimmer starts to swim again. The mind-body process is no different from stopping to rest while climbing a flight of stairs. You stop. You rest. You start to walk again. It really becomes just that simple.

For instance, if a competent swimmer unexpectedly falls into the water at a pool site, the only issue would be getting wet. But drown? Impossible! There is absolutely no danger involved. The competent swimmer instinctively swims back to the side of the pool. Suppose water goes up the competent swimmer's nose? So? It may cause some discomfort but it certainly cannot be considered life-threatening. What happens if the competent swimmer should get injured while falling? The competent swimmer will instinctively compensate for the injury just as a walker favors a sore foot after tripping. If the competent swimmer should bang his/her head while falling? Well, *that* is another story!

The non-competent swimmer, on the other hand, does not trust the mind-body connection. **The non-competent swimmer does not trust the mind to control the process.** The confidence of the non-competent swimmer is still shaky, which could mean that he/she is still in danger of panic. Although, the non-competent swimmer may have swimming skills, he/she is not in control of the biggest obstacle of all. The non-competent swimmer does not trust – *HIMSELF/ HERSELF.*

So what does the swimmer do when suddenly stopping to rest? Can the swimmer stop all movement? (I hope we all agree at this point that the answer is **NO!**) *It is time, then, for the learner to swim with head out of the water; whereby, the emphasis switches to **buoyancy and control,** as opposed to **streamlining and propulsion.*** It is time to learn the *"doggie paddle."*

INFANCY

Instinctively, man knows how to crawl. When my youngest son was born, I went into the baby viewing area and saw my son's head pressed up against the end of the plastic bassinet. Actually, it was "squished" up against the end of the bassinet. I was rather annoyed with the nurses for placing him in the bassinet this way. But, I did not argue and simply asked one of the nurses to place him back further. One half-hour later his head was pressed up against the bassinet again. This happened over and over again. How is this possible? Was the baby crawling ? I could not believe that a baby could crawl just hours after birth. *(I'm sure glad I did not argue with the nurses)*.

When we brought the baby home from the hospital, I placed him in the middle of our king sized bed. I was assured that it was perfectly safe. Twenty minutes later I went up to check him and found him hanging off the side of the bed. My heart was in my mouth. By the grace of God he did not fall off the bed. Somehow, I did not focus in on the process. I never connected the movement in the bassinet to the potential danger that was created when I placed the baby in the middle of the bed unattended. It sure makes a strong case for supervision. Doesn't it?

Programs which teach infants to swim tap into a baby's instinct to crawl. It is fascinating to watch how an infant's arms and legs interact with the resistance of water. It happens so naturally. Crawling in water is a rhythmic movement of the arms and legs that produces buoyancy and propulsion. Think for a moment about the origin of the name, "crawl" stroke. The crawl stroke is, in fact, modeled after instinctive crawling movements.

SIMILARITIES

- The body is horizontal.
- The movements of the arms and legs are rhythmic.
- The arm and leg movements alternate from side to side.
- Arm and leg movements are the same on both sides but move opposite and independent of each other.
- Both are two beat movements. That is, for each arm movement, there is a leg movement.
- The movements are continuous.

THE GOLDEN RULE FOR BEGINNERS

"If your head is in the water, your arms are out of the water. If your head is out of the water, your arms are in the water."

As was discussed earlier, I teach the **prone glide** followed by the **overhand arm stroke** followed by the **crawl stroke**. The focus for each of these strokes is on *streamlining.* The head is in the water at all times. Once the swimmer lifts the head, the legs begin to sink. The sinking of the legs creates *drag,* which restricts forward movement. The swimmer now has to be concerned about maintaining *buoyancy.* Buoyancy is maintained not only by keeping the legs moving but also by keeping the *arms moving in the water.*

HOW I TEACH THE "DOGGIE PADDLE"

Visualize for a second that you are on all fours as you would be when you are crawling. Lift the head the same way as you do as if you were about to crawl. **You look down and forward – not up!** Now superimpose yourself in the water. Once you do so, we know that your arms would be under the water and your head would be above the water. At this point, let us **streamline** our legs as we would while doing a **flutter** kick.

Notice that the chin is just above the water level. This is essential because raising the head too high creates pressure on the legs to sink. This causes drag. I tell my learners **to let the water touch your chin.** This command is very important. Allowing the water to touch the chin counteracts the tendency of the fearful learner to lift the head too far out of the water to the point of looking up. There is considerably less stress on the neck and shoulders and the head is better able to help counterbalance the legs. Once the head comes out of the water, the arms go in the water. The downside of lifting your head out of the water is that *streamlining* suffers. But, **you can see. You can breathe. You are buoyant. You are mobile.** *You are in control!*

The crawling arm movement on land is a constant forward motion. The arms continuously reach out. In the water the arms continuously *reach out* just as on land but they also *push down* and subsequently *pull back.* Combine this position and movement with a flutter kick and the swimmer should remain buoyant and mobile. *Voila!* **The swimmer is swimming with head out of the water.**

COMMANDS
- Place your arms under the water.
- Lift your head.   Let the water touch your chin.
- Reach out – Push down – Pull back.
- Kick – Kick – Kick.

ALTERNATE BEGINNER STROKE

I feel compelled at this time to reveal that not all of my learners LET GO. They will not give up the control and surrender to the feeling of disorientation. This does not prevent them, however, from practicing a flutter kick on a kickboard to the point of proficiency. If need be, they can use a buoyancy belt as an aid to coordinate the arm stroke with the flutter kick. Eventually, they *will* LET GO. The doggie paddle is an excellent stroke to use as an alternate beginner stroke for those students who just refuse to put their head in the water. In most cases it can be considered another "bait and switch" technique. Once the learner masters the doggie paddle, putting the head in the water usually is no longer such a big issue.

But just consider for a moment: the skills necessary to water-safe the learner are now in place. The next step is to stare the demon down. How? By practicing the crawl stroke and doggie paddle over and over again. Practice enhances proficiency. Proficiency enhances confidence. ***Confidence is the element that anchors the mind-body connection. Confidence persuades the mind to trust the body to act and not panic.*** The most wonderful part of all is that once the learning process is in full gear the learner is going to want to practice. Success is the greatest motivator of all.

ALWAYS KEEP THE ELBOW HIGHER THAN THE HAND

The learner's elbow should be always higher than the hand. This is a fundamental principle in both the doggie paddle and the overhand arm strokes. The doggie paddle is modeled after how a dog swims. Have you ever watched a dog swim? The dog's knee is always higher than the paw. Dogs swim instinctively yet there are dogs who either cannot swim or swim with great difficulty. These dogs lift their paws out of the water which means that the paw is now higher than the knee. Dogs that swim with proficiency keep their paws lower than their knees at all times.

In the case of the front leg of a dog, this would be the human equivalent of an elbow and a hand. The same rules apply. *Keeping the elbow higher than the hand is necessary to execute an effective arm stroke.*

LEARNING TO SWIM AT ORCHARD BEACH

Walking along the water's edge at Orchard Beach, I often meet students, former students, and parents of students I have taught. Invariably, the subject of learning how to swim comes up. Very often I am asked what a child or sibling who is a non-swimmer can do that day to begin learning how to swim.

Let me describe my favorite suggestion, which is applicable most anywhere:

The water at Orchard Beach is calm and except at low tide, the change in water depth from the water's edge to deep water is very gradual. Starting in shallow water, I have the learner begin crawling toward the deep water with the arms only. The legs should be straight and together. The learner's chin should be touching the water.

As the learner goes deeper into the water, the body becomes elevated by the water. The effectiveness and power of the arm movement will now be governed more and more by the resistance of the water. By the time the learner reaches a depth just above the knees, the body will begin to be suspended in the water. The learner quickly realizes that it is the arm movement used as the body is suspended in the water that governs the effectiveness of the arm stroke. The learner can now take risks, easily recover, and experience the feel of swimming with the arms in safe shallow water.

DEEP WATER – STARTING ON TOP

Swimming in deep water for the first time is a tremendous thrill. Not only are you staring the demon down, you are chasing the demon away. Nobody can do it for you which only embellishes the delight. It is fun. It is controlled. It is safe. From a teaching standpoint this is the part I relish the most. The mission is complete. The mind and body connect.

But let us not forget that the learner is over his/her head and could suddenly panic and go blank. It does happen. It is important to remember that the initial period of swimming in deep water is a time requiring extreme caution and maximum supervision. The teacher/swimmer must be in a position to intervene immediately. Personally, I am always in the water right next to my learners during this initial period. I start my young learners in about five feet of water. It is usually over their heads, but not mine. If my learner begins to panic, I immediately place my hands under the learner's armpits and lift the youngster out of the water. There is no way that I am going to allow swimming in deep water for the first time to become a negative experience for the learner. It may be an unsuccessful experience, but never a negative experience. The learner must feel safe and protected at all times. It must be said, however, that it is quite rare when I have to physically intervene in this way because I do not allow beginners to swim in deep water until they are ready.

PREPARATION

• The learner swimming in deep water for the first time should be given a specific distance goal.

• The learner should be reminded that he/she is starting on top of the water and should not stop for any reason. It is much harder to swim if you let your legs sink since, if that happens, the learner would have to *streamline* in order to continue swimming. Learning to streamline the body from a vertical position in the water is not our aim at the moment.

• The learner should take two deep breaths before positioning the face down in the water and holding the breath. There are rare occasions when I allow my learners to swim in deep water with their heads out of the water using a doggie paddle. It is more efficient, however, to swim with the head in the water and by this stage of progress, the learner is usually not resistant to putting head in the water.

• It is important to make sure that there is no other swimmer or obstacle that could cut off or in any other way interfere with the learner's path. Such interference could break his/her concentration and cause panic.

• This exercise is intended as a confidence builder. Some learners may want to continue practicing in deep water. That is fine. But, each attempt at swimming in deep water at this point must be done with permission.

• Communication is important. The learner has to know that each attempt at swimming in deep water must be carefully supervised.

BUOYANCY IN PLACE

So now the learner can swim on top of the water from side to side. But can we be assured that the learner will have the poise to remain calm and not panic in a situation that is not controlled? Suppose, for instance, the learner is in deep water suddenly and unexpectedly. The learner is momentarily disoriented and is over his/her head. Is the learner water-safe at this point? *Maybe.*

The critical issue is that the learner has only demon-strated swimming proficiency while starting on top of the water. The learner is already *streamlined*. Let's call this **horizontal proficiency**. But what if the learner is starting to swim with the legs under the water? Now the learner has to first kick the legs to the surface and streamline before being able to propel the body forward. Let's call this **vertical proficiency**.

It is much easier to swim starting with your legs on top of the water. Usually, the learner's legs are on top of the water when he/she is hanging onto the side of the pool or using some other kind of prop. The situation is controlled. But what if the situation is not controlled as when you fall into the water suddenly and unexpectedly?

Now is the time to use buoyancy-in-place skills. Buoyancy-in-place is the ability to keep your head out of water while at the same time rhythmically moving your arms and legs in place in the water.

HIGHLIGHTS

- Try to keep the legs at a 30° angle under the water. The more vertical you are the more the legs will have a tendency to pull you under the water.
- Spread the arms and legs apart. In this way you are spreading out your body weight.
- Keep your arms extended in front of the body. Never laterally! Counterbalance the legs.
- Keep the head down. Don't look up. Let the water touch your chin.
- Alternately bend the knees and don't forget to point the toes back. The kick should now start at the knee and not at the hip. With the legs bent lower in the water, the knees have more leverage. **Remember, we are work-ing more on buoyancy than on propulsion.** A learner can now *slide* the bent knee forward and use more force-

ful kicks. The kicks will push the learner up and forward.
- Execute the Doggie Paddle arm stroke keeping the arms
  well under the surface of the water.

SCULLING

The approach to our arm movements up until now
has been *linear*. That is, the learner has been encouraged to
pull the water straight back. Pulling the water straight back
"works," and is an effective method of executing the doggie
paddle arm stroke. A more efficient arm movement, however, is to move the arm in an **"in-out-in"** pattern as we
pull the arm back. The more water we can grab and hold on
to maximizes the resistance of water.

We briefly mentioned the *sculling* motion when discussing the overhand arm stroke. I prefer to allow my learners to do what comes naturally. As the learner builds up
confidence the various parts of the body begin to relax and
an "in-out-in" pattern begins to develop naturally in response
to the resistance of the water. The learner instinctively begins to realize that the more water he/she can grab and hold
on to, the more effective the doggie paddle arm stroke becomes. Be assured, the body responds rhythmically in kind
as the mind-body connection develops.

Learning to swim is no different than learning how
to dance. As we build up confidence and become more
comfortable with the steps and turns, our body responds
rhythmically to the music. Our various body parts fine tune
the movement and we are limited only by our God-given
talents. Swimming is no different since the confident swimmer responds to water just like the dancer responds to music.

VERTICAL TO HORIZONTAL

When a swimmer falls into the water, there will be a
tendency to float up toward the surface. Rarely will the

swimmer end up vertical in the water. The air in the lungs and the resistance of water will push the swimmer up toward the surface initially. Remember that inaction, lifting the head and bending the knees will cause the legs to sink. **The at-risk swimmer must** *streamline* **immediately by placing his/her arms in front of the shoulders, bring the legs together, straighten the legs, point the toes back and kick the legs. In other words, "Don't think! Do!"**

If on the other hand, the learner is inactive, lifts the head, bends the knees, or tries to reach for the bottom with the feet to stand, the learner will now become vertical in the water. The learner, at this point, is better off extending the arms in front of the shoulders, sliding the knees forward and using **buoyancy-in-place** techniques. Once the learner gets the legs close to a 30° angle under the water the learner can now **streamline** and swim to safety. If the learner chooses, he/she can crawl quite effectively through the water using buoyancy in place techniques. **Buoyancy in place can be likened to the instinctive crawl movements of an infant.**

DEEP WATER – STOPPING

An effective confidence builder at this point is to have the learner start swimming a crawl stroke from the side of the pool in deep water. This drill should be practiced in a depth of 4-5' so that you are in a position to intervene if necessary. The learner should take three overhand arm strokes – **stop** – execute buoyancy in place – put the head back in the water – continue swimming to the other side of the pool.

THE YOUNG BOY

Walking along the water's edge at Orchard Beach this past summer, I observed a young boy about 8 or 9 years of age who was in the water over his head. Orchard Beach, as you may recall, is on Long Island Sound. The swimming conditions are more akin to a bay rather than to an ocean.

For the most part, it is quite calm. On this particular day, there was an off-shore breeze and an outgoing tide current which made swimming away from shore slightly easier. The boy was attempting to swim back against the same wind and current that assisted him as he swam out to deep water. Swimming back toward shore was now somewhat more difficult. He had to swim back 10-15 feet to shore in order to stand.

I first noticed the youngster as he was beginning to swim in toward shore. There was a slight "chop" in the water which caused the water to splash mildly in his face. In effect, it was a rather typical as opposed to a "man against the elements" situation. He was doing a "universal" stroke – flailing his arms as he was turning his head from side to side. His head was too high and too much of his body was under the water for him to make any headway.

His next strategy was to place his arms in the water and begin a doggie paddle/buoyancy-in-place technique. He was buoyant, but once again he was making no headway. (I was sure that he was trying to catch his breath as well.) Finally, he put his head down in the water, extended his arms out in front of his shoulders, placed legs together, pointed toes back, and kicked his way to shore using a flutter kick. It was a prone glide with a flutter kick. Very effective!

Situations such as these are very typical but normally go unnoticed. Certainly, they are never analyzed. In reality, a great deal happened in that 15-20 seconds. Let's look at the process. The swimmer probably could have made it back to safety using a universal stroke if the water were perfectly calm. The slight "chop" in the water from the wind and current caused him to raise his head higher than normal. This caused his legs to sink too far under the water. He wisely placed his arms in the water using a buoyancy-in-place technique to rest and catch his breath. He extended his arms in front of his shoulders, took a deep breath, placed his head in the water and kicked himself to safety using a flutter kick. *He streamlined!* What this boy lacked in swimming skills, he made up for with good water competency instincts.

It was obvious that the boy was in control of the situation. His mind commanded his body. He continuously assessed and planned different strategies. He remained focused without even a hint of panic with his mind and body connecting. He may not have had any real swimming skills but one sensed that this boy had spent some time in the water. This is not always the case however.

THE TEENAGER AND THE BRIDGE

One day I was walking along the Bronx mainland across from City Island near the City Island bridge. The distance between City Island and the Bronx mainland at that point is approximately 200 yards. There were several teenage boys about to jump near the middle of the bridge. Actually this location was in the boat traffic lanes. Very dangerous! The height of the bridge was approximately 20-25 feet. There was a very strong current running and wind blowing away from the bridge at the point where the boys were preparing to jump.

The first boy jumped into the water. Using a "universal" stroke, he began swinging his head and arms from side to side, but he was trying to swim against the strong wind and current. The water was splashing in his face. Instinctively, he lifted his head higher, forcing his legs to sink further under the water. Compounding the problem, the strong current was causing him to be pushed away from his destination. He became more and more frantic. Each attempt at a forward movement proved fruitless. None of his "friends" jumped in the water to help him. **Panic set in!**

Two men in a 23-foot powerboat saw the teenager in trouble and tried to rescue him. The problem was that they approached the boy running with the wind and current and nearly ran him over. They were fortunate since such mistakes with a vessel often have tragic results. Finally, a young man from the boat rental dock on City Island briskly paddled a rowboat to the victim and rescued him.

If the teenager would have been a more skilled swimmer, he would have realized that he had to *streamline* his body. Obviously, either he did not know how to *streamline* or did not realize he had to *streamline.* Up until this point he probably was getting by with a marginal universal stroke. His swimming experience was obviously limited to safe calm waters. I am sure this fellow could jump off a high board at a pool and never experience a problem. Under those circumstances, the activity is quite safe. But, jumping off the City Island bridge in a running tide? No way! This young man was clearly out of his league.

If he would have been one of my students, I would have expected him to instinctively take a deep breath, put his head in the water, use an overhand arm stroke, flutter kick and take 10-15 strong strokes to safety – very "doable." Even better, it is my hope that one of my students would have had enough sense not to jump off a bridge in the first place!

THE LESSON

Sometimes a little knowledge is a dangerous thing. The teenager was probably "showing-off". He could "swim" but was not water competent. Even if the water were calm, he could easily have been run over by a boat. For his age, the young nine-year-old described earlier appeared to be much more water competent than the teenager. He instinctively knew that he had to *streamline* when the water splashed him in the face. The teenager, on the other hand, never made the connection. He lifted his head higher in the water when the water began splashing him in the face. Lifting his head higher caused his legs to sink further under the water, creating more *drag.* I am not suggesting that the young boy had the skills necessary to save himself against a strong wind and current. **I am simply saying that he had better instincts!**

10
A DROWNING SCENARIO

I am standing by the edge of the pool. All of a sudden I am falling – falling into the water. I reach out to break the fall. I hit the water. My body is on top of the water. What is happening? Some water went up my nose. My eyes are not seeing like they normally do. I dare not rub them. I am so confused and disoriented. I feel out of control. I lift my head as high and back as possible trying to catch a breath. I reach and grab at the water to my sides and try to push my head above water to breathe. But the water cannot always lift me. I am sinking. I cannot touch the bottom. I need some air, but I cannot catch a breath. The horror of it all is that I am going to drown!"

At long last, the time has come to complete the mission. So *what does an at-risk swimmer do* when faced with a sudden unexpected occurrence, such as being over the head in deep water? Obviously, the answer is to swim to *safety*. But before we can answer the question of *what does the at-risk swimmer do*, we must first answer the question of *what does the at-risk swimmer not do?*

DON'T STOP UNTIL YOU DROP
The at-risk swimmer must not stop swimming until absolutely certain that he/she is no longer in deep water. The swimmer **must not** *trust the eyes* to make this determi-

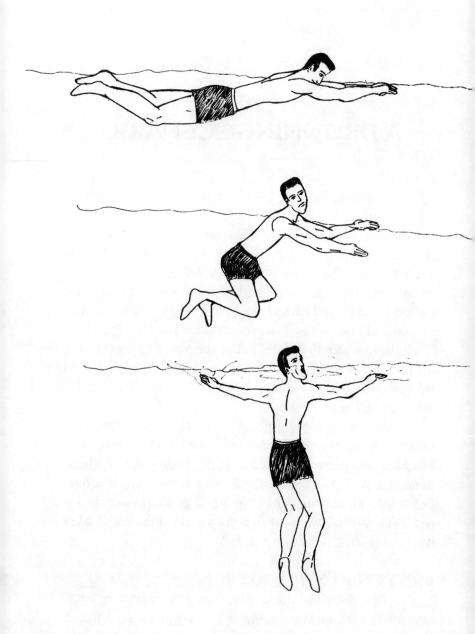

nation. The eyes are an unreliable indicator of water depth. The danger of deep water remains until the swimmer reaches *something solid or buoyant to hold on to.* The swimmer should keep swimming until he/she reaches the side of a pool, the side of a dock, or the side of a boat. If at a beach, the at-risk swimmer must keep on swimming toward the shore until the *hands touch the bottom.* Only then is he/she assured that there is no longer any danger of drowning.

Secondly, the at-risk swimmer must avoid the instinct to bend the knees, lift the head, and reach for the bottom with the toes in order to stand. Remember that this instinct, even though counter-productive, is real and must be reckoned with. The ability to overcome the **instinct** to bend the knees, lift the head, and reach for the bottom with the toes, causing the swimmer to become **vertical** in the water, could literally be the *difference between life and death*. Propulsion can only be accomplished when the body is **horizontal** in the water. Now the at-risk swimmer must work considerably harder to *counterbalance* and *streamline* the body in order to propel the body. *The body, when suddenly suspended vertically in deep water, wreaks havoc on the fragile mind-body connection of the at-risk swimmer.*

Third, never take your arms out of the water. If there is air in the lungs, the body will be buoyant. The issue is how much of the buoyant body is under the water versus on top of the water. *The position of the arms, legs and head in relation to the water will determine the level of buoyancy.* By taking the arms out of water, more of the body goes under the water and the head, which is of special importance – sinks.

The arms give stability to the body. Not only must the arms be in the water to *stabilize* and *buoy* the body, they must *counterbalance*, *streamline,* and *propel* the body through the water. *The at-risk swimmer must never forget that the arms must always be in the water and extended in front of the shoulders in order to be in a position to elevate and propel the body through the water.* Once the body is *streamlined*, the swimmer can execute the swimming stroke of choice.

NEVER EXTEND THE ARMS LATERALLY

Drowning victims have a tendency to extend their arms laterally and push down on the water to catch a breath. Trying to catch a breath this way is exhausting and inhibits streamlining and counterbalancing. The legs are prevented from executing an effective kick and pull the victim under the water.

WHAT TO *DO!*   *REACT!*

KICK

The at-risk swimmer must instinctively move the legs immediately. It is the weight of the legs that causes the swimmer to become vertical and pulls the rest of the body under the water. Instinctively moving the legs right away empowers the at risk swimmer to feel in control and take charge of the situation immediately. The mind is in control of the body.

COMMAND

If ever I see one of my learners beginning to become frightened, my command is always *"Kick," "Kick," "Kick,"* reminding everyone that once the legs are counterbalanced and streamlined, swimming is easy.

The intent of a command is to produce a conditioned reflex response by the at-risk swimmer. The at-risk swimmer focuses on the solution, not on the problem. Please note that the command is one word "KICK!" There is no reason for phrases, sentences or explanations. Secondly, the command should be given in a commanding voice – never an hysterical one. The voice should convey to the at-risk swimmer an implicit belief in the command itself.

MOVE THE ARMS

Immediately extend the arms in front of the shoulders to counterbalance and streamline the body. Never laterally! Execute the arm movement of choice.

KEEP THE HEAD DOWN

The at-risk swimmer must avoid the temptation to lift the head too far out of the water. A frightened swimmer will instinctively lift the head too high in order to take a breath. Lifting the head too high is a kind of a negative **counterbalancing.** The legs compensate by going further under the water. **The swimmer should tilt the head slightly forward and allow the water to touch the chin.**

MOVEMENTS THAT EMPOWER

PRONE GLIDE WITH A KICK
The swimmer:
- ° Takes a deep breath.
- ° Places the head in the water with the face looking down and forward.
- ° Extends the arms in front of the shoulders, angled in, never out.
- ° Brings the legs together.
- ° Straightens the legs.
- ° Points the toes back.
- ° Executes the flutter kick.
- ° Kicks to safety with arms extended in front of the shoulders.

OVERHAND ARM STROKE
The swimmer:
- ° Takes a deep breath.
- ° Places the head in the water.
- ° Brings the legs together.
- ° Straightens the legs.
- ° Points the toes back.
- ° Extends the arms in front of the shoulders, angled in, never out.
- ° Pulls back with one arm.
- ° Executes an overhand arm stroke.
- ° Swims to safety.

The decision to use a *flutter* kick with the overhand arm stroke should be based on whether or not the kick *enhances* or *impedes* movement. Are the arms and legs moving in *synch?*

DOGGIE PADDLE
The swimmer:
- ° Places the arms under the water.
- ° Lifts the head but lets the water touch the chin.
- ° Uses the arms to alternately reach out under the water – pushes the water down – pulls the water back.
- ° Executes a flutter kick.
- ° Swims to safety.

BUOYANCY IN PLACE
The swimmer:
- ° Tries to get legs into a 30° angle under water.
- ° Spreads arms and legs apart.
- ° Keeps arms extended in front of body.
- ° Keeps head down – does not look up - lets water touch the chin.

° Bends knees slightly and points toes back.
° Originates an alternating kick from the knee. Just as in crawling on land, the knee slides forward as the arm reaches forward.
° Uses arms to alternately reach out under the water – pushes water down – pulls water back.
° Catches breath, swims to safety or plans a course of action.

Buoyancy in place should be used if the at-risk swimmer is *vertical* in the water or in situations requiring an *action plan*.

CLOTHING

Clothing severely inhibits the rhythm of any stroke. Clothing gets waterlogged and adds considerable *resistance* to the effectiveness of arm strokes and kicks. Shoes and boots can make an effective kick almost impossible. *There are no solutions to this problem other than wearing a life vest in any situation where it is possible to end up suddenly and unexpectedly in deep water.* Life vests that are made today are light, comfortable and functional with pockets and other accessories. I strongly recommend them.

"JOHNNY, GET THE OAR!"

When I was a young boy, I went for a ride on my Uncle Herb's boat with my father and my Uncle George. Uncle George was my father's brother. Uncle Herb was married to my mother's sister, Aunt Beatrice. Uncle Herb was under the impression that Uncle George could not swim.

Uncle Herb's boat was moored about 100 yards off shore. We rowed to his boat in a small rowboat, a dinghy. My father and my two uncles were big men and only one adult and myself could safely fit in the dinghy at one time. It was my job to transport the dinghy back and forth. It was late afternoon and it was time to return to shore. The weather was relatively calm.

When traveling in a small boat such as a dinghy, often the best way to keep your clothes dry and out of the way is to wear them. I put on my pants over my bathing suit and put on a tee-shirt, sweat shirt, socks and sneakers.

I climbed into the dinghy and sat in the middle seat so that I could row to shore. Uncle George climbed into the back seat. He felt that he should be the one rowing since he was the adult. I told Uncle George that it was okay for me to row but he insisted that he should be the one rowing. We attempted to switch seats and the boat suddenly tipped over. We both ended up in the water!

Uncle Herb immediately went to assist Uncle George. My father yelled, "Johnny, get the oar!" The oar was drifting away. My father then focused his energy on trying to recover the small dinghy and later helping Uncle George climb back onto the boat.

I swam after the oar, but my ability to swim was greatly inhibited by the clothing I was wearing. The more I swam, the more I became weighted down by my water-soaked clothing. My sneakers made it almost impossible to kick effectively. My swimming became more and more labored. I suddenly realized that I could barely swim. Even worse, nobody realized my dilemma! In my family environment, my ability to swim was taken for granted. Swimming after an oar was no different than asking me to run around the corner and buy a quart of milk. Eventually, I reached the oar and struggled to push it back to the boat.

The above experience was another milestone in my personal water-competency awareness. If I had to jump in the water to save someone in a difficult rescue, no way would anything be on my feet and I would wear as little as possible.

DISTRESS vs DROWNING

There is an important differentiation that should be made at this time. A person who can keep his/her head above water and wave or call for help is in a *distress* situation – not a *drowning* situation. There is a very big difference. A person who is in *distress* is able to breathe, provided that he/she remains in some kind of rhythmic movement pattern with arms and legs.

A person who is *drowning* is literally suffocating to death. It is impossible for a drowning victim to yell or wave for help since instinctively all of his/her energy is being expended on trying to breathe. The drowning victim has, on average, 20-60 seconds before he/she suffocates and drowns.

RESCUE

The focus of *Teacher/Swimmer* is on how the at-risk swimmer saves himself/herself. Rescue involves rendering assistance to a person in danger of drowning. Anyone rendering assistance to a person in danger of drowning should also understand that the rescue should not endanger the life of the rescuer, as well as others.

FACTORS TO CONSIDER

Location: Is it a pool? Is it a lake?
Is it the side of a boat?
How far is the victim from safety?
Number, size and skill level of drowning victim(s).
Number, size and skill level of rescuer(s).

OPTIONS AND PARAMETERS

° Is there a lifeguard? Other bathers? Don't waste time. ***Call for help!***
° Is there *something that floats* nearby that can hold up the drowning victim? A life preserver ? A cushion? A ring buoy. Either throw it or bring

it to the victim. A rescuer can wear a life pre-server and bring some kind of floatation device to the victim *(be sure both of you can return to safety)*.

° Is there a *long pole*? – an oar? – a paddle? – a fishing pole? – a pool skimmer? – something you can use to reach out to the victim without physically leaving safety?

° *Talk to the victim*. Give commands such as *"kick!" "kick!" "kick!"*

° Will the *clothing* you are wearing impede an in-water rescue?

Try to think! Try not to react impulsively! This is no simple task for the inexperienced rescuer - especially when rescuing a loved one.

The SCISSORS KICK

The *scissors* kick is the leg movement used more than any other leg movement for rescue. The *scissors* kick is also known as the side stroke kick.

The *scissors* kick is used while swimming on the side. *While swimming on the side, you can keep the mouth out of water and continuously breathe at all times.* As opposed to the *flutter* kick, which is a continuous alternating up and down movement of the legs, the *scissors* kick involves **three** leg movements. The movements are:

1. Bring knees up and together.
2. Spread legs apart.
3. Squeeze the water by bringing legs together.

Propulsion is achieved by compressing the water between the legs as the legs come together. By way of example, the scissors kick movement rhythm can be loosely compared to a bellows when stoking a fire. You spread the

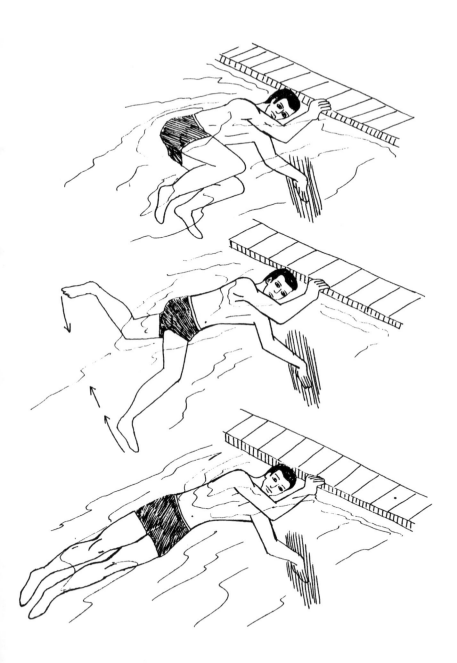

handles apart allowing the bellows to fill up with air. You squeeze the handles compressing the air in the bellows. The air is forced into the fire. Once the bellows is out of air, you allow the bellows to fill up with air and begin the process all over again.

POWER
The power leg in the scissors kick is the leg furthest under the water. Most swimmers have a favorite power leg. My preferred power leg is my right leg. Therefore, I always execute a scissors kick on my right side, never on my left.

HOW I TEACH THE *SCISSORS* KICK
- Have the learner hold onto the side of the pool.
- Hold the learner's feet.
- Push feet forward, forcing the learner's knees up and together toward the waist.
- Spread the legs apart.
- Squeeze the legs together as you would a scissors, **stressing the power of the bottom leg.**
- Use the commands: *"Up!" "Out!" "Squeeze!"*

ADULT-CHILD RESCUE
Since most rescue situations for a *teacher/swimmer* involve an adult rescuing a child for short distances, an effective technique is as follows:

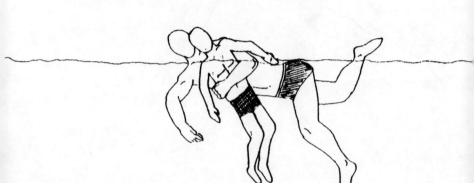

- Swim to the victim.
- Firmly grab the victim below the chest but above the waist with one arm and lift the victim's head and shoulders out of the water.
- Rotate your body to the side.
- Execute a scissors kick.
- Simultaneously extend and pull back on your underwater arm as you squeeze your legs together.
- Continue this stroke until you reach safety.

If you cannot effectively execute a scissors kick , it may be more "doable" to pull or push the victim to safety. This could involve going under the water and pushing the victim simultaneously up and to the side.

DANGEROUS CLICHÉ: "RELAX! DON'T PANIC!"

Very often the above sage advice is given to beginning swimmers when faced with a drowning situation. I was discussing this expression with my nephew, Gary, who is now 32 and took swimming lessons in high school. When faced with a drowning situation, he interpreted this expression as meaning that you should remain motionless in the water.

In essence, you should be doing the same in water as you would do on land. You stop! You process! You assess! You plan! Meanwhile, the laws of gravity are busy at work. Nobody mentions to you that while you are *"relaxing,"* you had better keep your legs and arms in some kind of rhythmic movement or else your body will begin to *sink* vertically. **You are in water – not on land. In effect, the phrase "relax don't panic" can be misleading, as my nephew learned. But perhaps the expression should be:** *"Relax!" "Don't Panic!" "Move!"*

FINAL THOUGHTS

There is no substitute for *CAUTION*. There is no substitute for *SUPERVISION*. There is no substitute for *SENSITIVITY*. There is no substitute for *EMPATHY*. There is no substitute for *PRACTICE*. There is no substitute for *EXPERIENCE*. Enjoy the new world that has been opened to you – you, the *TEACHER/SWIMMER*.